Collins

LITTLE BOOKS

T0328055

CARD GAMES

HarperCollins Publishers
Westerhill Road
Bishopbriggs
Glasgow
G64 2QT

HarperCollins Publishers
Macken House, 39/40 Mayor Street
Upper, Dublin 1, D01 C9W8, Ireland

First Edition 2018

15 14 13 12 11 10 9

© HarperCollins Publishers 2018
© Diagram Visual Information 2000,
2004

ISBN 978-0-00-830653-3

Collins® is a registered trademark
of HarperCollins Publishers Limited
www.collins.co.uk

Editor: Ian Brookes

Typeset by
Davidson Publishing Solutions

Printed and bound India

A catalogue record for this book is
available from the British Library

All rights reserved. No part of this book
may be reproduced, stored in a retrieval
system, or transmitted in any form or
by any means, electronic, mechanical,
photocopying, recording or otherwise,
without the prior permission in writing
of the Publisher. This book is sold
subject to the conditions that it shall
not, by way of trade or otherwise, be
lent, re-sold, hired out or otherwise
circulated without the Publisher's prior
consent in any form of binding or cover
other than that in which it is published
and without a similar condition
including this condition being imposed
on the subsequent purchaser.

HarperCollins does not warrant that
www.collins.co.uk or any other website
mentioned in this title will be provided
uninterrupted, that any website will be
error-free, that defects will be corrected,
or that the website or the server that
makes it available are free of viruses
or bugs. For full terms and conditions
please refer to the site terms provided
on the website.

MIX
Paper | Supporting
responsible forestry
FSC™ C007454

This book contains FSC™ certified paper and other controlled
sources to ensure responsible forest management.

For more information visit: www.harpercollins.co.uk/green

Contents

Introduction

Card playing has been a popular pastime among young and old for more than 500 years. This long history and the enormous variety of card games that exist, give card playing its great potential as a plentiful source of entertainment for all ages.

Collins Little Book of Card Games is a fascinating full-colour guide to the rules and strategies for more than 40 exciting games, from all-fives to war, including the likes of euchre, canasta, pinochle and rummy. There's something for everyone – beginner and expert alike. Also included is an easy-to-use, complete glossary of important terms used in card playing. And with each game, you'll find the answers to those inevitable debates over rules and scoring.

Most importantly, the book provides detailed instructions and play-by-play diagrams – illustrating techniques and surefire strategies – that will turn even the novice card player into an expert.

A history of playing cards

The exact time and place when card games were invented cannot be known for certain. However, it is fairly clear that playing cards – just like paper, clocks and fireworks – started life in China, and that the first cards were produced before AD 1000. These cards probably featured symbols that represented coins, and would have looked more like modern-day dominoes than the cards in modern deck.

From China, the use of playing cards spread through Asia, and it was the Mamelukes, a group of soldiers who had established a powerful empire in Egypt, who introduced playing cards to Europe around 1370. The earliest European packs had 52 cards divided into four suits, just like a standard modern pack, although the designs on the cards were markedly different from what we know today.

THE DEVELOPMENT OF THE FOUR SUITS

The playing cards that came from Egypt contained designs influenced by Islamic culture, with cups, swords, coins and polo sticks. As cards became popular across Europe, different countries would produce variations on these designs that made more sense to the local people. Thus the polo stick – which was not known in Europe at the time – was transformed into a baton in southern Europe, while in Germany the symbols of acorns, leaves, hearts and bells eventually became standard.

At this point playing cards were hand-painted, and so they were expensive to produce and could only be afforded by rich people. However, around 1480, French manufacturers realised that by making the patterns on the cards simpler, the cards would be cheaper to produce. They came up with four simple shapes that could be drawn using a stencil: the trefoil (the modern club), the diamond, the heart, and the pike-head (the modern spade).

The new French designs made playing cards available to many more people, and the French pack has gradually became accepted as the international standard. However, there are still regional variations that can be dated back to the earlier suit designs, such as bells being used as a suit in Germany and Switzerland or cups being a suit in Italy and Spain.

OTHER CHANGES IN THE PACK

The idea of having thirteen cards of a different value in each suit was already present when cards arrived in Europe. The one significant difference was that the early sets had three male court cards: a king, a knight and a servant. The queen was later added instead of the servant and was given a value between the knight and the king, and the knight was also renamed as the 'knave' or 'jack'.

The pack has changed in other ways over the years too. Until around 1800 the backs of the cards were plain white. This meant that the cards could be discoloured and even deliberately marked, and by remembering these marks a dishonest player might be able to know the value of a card that was face down or in an opponent's hand. To stop this from happening, manufacturers took to printing coloured designs on the backs of the cards.

Another relatively late innovation to make playing card games fairer was the idea of adding the number and suit of each card in the corner as well as in the middle of the card. Before this was done, players had to hold a card away from the rest of their hand to see what it was, and this might expose the card to an opponent's view. But from the 1860s the value of each card was printed in the corner, and so players could hold their cards together in a tight fan and get a quick view of all the cards in a hand without giving much away.

Around the same time, card manufacturers began to include two jokers in the pack. These cards could be used to stand in for a lost or damaged card so that a pack did not become useless if one card went missing. However, they were also accommodated into various games so that a player with a joker could use it to represent any card in the deck. The fact that the jokers are a late addition to the deck accounts for the fact that not many of the established card games use them.

TYPES OF CARD GAME

The earliest card games seem to have involved a series of rounds in which each player played one card and the card with the highest value won that round or 'trick'. These games could be made more interesting by having a 'trump' suit, so that a card of that suit would automatically beat any card of the other suits.

Early trick-taking games included 'triumph' and 'ombre' (which introduced the idea of having an auction to decide the trump suit before the hand was played rather than cutting a card to decide the trumps). The game of triumph later evolved into whist, which was widely played in coffee houses and drawing rooms in the eighteenth and nineteenth centuries. In the twentieth century contract bridge overtook whist and became established as the most popular trick-taking game among expert players.

While trick-taking games have remained popular, card games that work in other ways have also emerged. There is, for example, a whole family of games that involve arranging the cards in a hand to form matching sets and sequences. These games probably derive from 'conquain', which was developed in Mexico in the nineteenth century. Probably the best-known game of this kind is rummy, while canasta is a more complex variation on the same theme that involves two packs of cards.

Another distinctive type of game is patience, where a player has no opponents but must try to sort the pack into a pattern while being restricted to certain moves.

This sort of card game is first recorded in northern Europe in the 1780s and probably developed from the practice of dealing out cards into patterns as a way of predicting the future.

The fact that so many different types of game can be played using the same pack shows just what a remarkably flexible invention playing cards are. The games included in this book have been chosen to offer something for everyone and for every occasion. They include games that are simple to learn and that everyone can play (such as snap and war) alongside complicated games that require players to use subtlety and strategy (such as canasta and cribbage). They include games for one player (clock, solitaire), games for two players matched head-to-head (bezique, gin rummy), and games that can be enjoyed by larger groups (hearts, Newmarket). Some of the games require great skill while others are entirely dependent on chance. While many of the games in the book are played quite widely, there are also a few games that are not so well-known, so that even experienced card players will find something new here.

All fives

A game for two or three players similar to whist.

CARDS
The standard deck of 52 cards is used with ace ranking high. A suit is assigned trumps which outranks all other suits. A set of two or three cards, one from each player in turn, is called a trick.

AIM
Individuals score points by trumping tricks.

PREPARING
Paper and pencil are needed for scoring. The player with the highest cut becomes dealer. Anyone may shuffle the pack before the cuts are made.

DEALING
The dealer shuffles the pack. Rotating clockwise and starting from the player on their left, they deal six cards in packets of three cards face down to each player. The next card is turned face up to assign trumps.

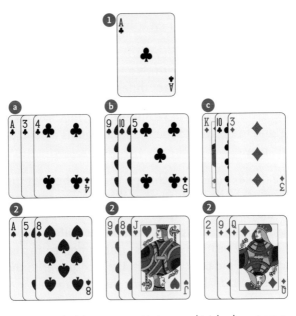

1 Trumped tricks

a Ace clubs wins

b 5 clubs wins

c 10 clubs wins

2 Untrumped tricks do not score

The dealer reveals the first trump suit.

By saying 'stand', the player to the left of the dealer accepts the assigned trumps and play begins. They say 'I beg' if instead they want different trumps assigned.

If the dealer decides to retain trumps, they say 'take one' and the player to their left then gains a point and starts play.

If the dealer decides to change trumps, they put the upcard aside, deal a further packet of three cards to each player and turn up the next card to assign the new trumps. If the upcard is the same suit as before, the dealer repeats this process until a new trump is assigned. If the pack runs out, the next player to their left becomes dealer and begins the deal again.

PLAYING

The player to the left of the dealer places one card face up on the table. Players each follow suit with one card. The trick is taken by the person playing the highest ranking card; they lead for the next trick.

SCORING
Tricks are all turned face up at the end of the round. Only tricks containing certain trump cards score points, as follows:

Ace	4 points
K	3 points
Q	2 points
J	1 point
10	10 points
5	5 points

WINNING THE GAME
The player first reaching a score of 61 or more is the winner.

Sometimes called setback, this variation of seven-up is particularly popular in the USA.

PLAYERS
Two to seven people can play.

CARDS
A standard deck of 52 cards is used. Ace ranks high. A trick is two to seven cards, one played by each person in turn.

AIM
Individuals try to score points to win the game. Although seven points is the standard game, players can play for 10, 11 or 21 points if they agree.

PREPARING
Pencil and paper are needed for scoring.

DEALING
The dealer – chosen by the highest cut – shuffles the

cards and deals two packets of three cards, face down, to each player.

BIDDING
The player on the dealer's left either declares pass or bids to make a score of one, two, three or four. The last, a slam, is also known as 'shoot the moon' or 'smudge'.

The next player clockwise then passes or bids and so on. Players must always bid higher than the previous bidder, although the dealer may choose to take the last bid over. The person holding the highest bid is known as the pitcher.

PLAYING
The pitcher begins by playing one card face up, which also assigns trumps for that deal. Other players must follow the trump suit or make a discard. The trick is won by the highest ranking card and claimed by that player, who then leads for the next trick.

When the leading card is a plain suit, players can follow suit or play a trump card. If they cannot do either, they must discard one card.

SCORING
If the pitcher's score is equal to or greater than their bid, they keep their score. If they have failed, they lose the number of points they bid, which may leave them with a minus score.

All other players score according to the cards they hold in their tricks.

Highest trump card	1 point
Lowest trump card	1 point
J of trumps	1 point
Aces	4 points
Ks	3 points
Qs	2 points
Js	1 point
10s	10 points
Highest total card value	1 point

WINNING THE GAME

The person who first makes 7 or more points (or 10, 11 or 21, as agreed) wins the game. When players tie, points are counted in the order of high, low, J and then game. The pitcher always wins when they tie with another player.

An exciting, easy game for two to six players in which winning depends largely on luck.

CARDS
For two or three players, a standard deck of cards. It does not matter if a few cards are missing. Four or more players need approximately two packs.

AIM
To win all the cards in an agreed time limit.

DEALING
All the cards are dealt out one at a time; the deal might not be even. Nobody is allowed to look at their cards, which each player collects in a face-down pile.

PLAYING
The person on the dealer's left begins by placing their top card face up in the centre of the table. In turn, clockwise, each player adds a card to the centre pile until someone turns up an ace, J, Q or K (court card).

The player so doing demands payment from the next player as follows:

a	For an ace	four cards
b	For a K	three cards
c	For a Q	two cards
d	For a J	one card

The payment cards are turned over and put on the central pile.

If a payment card is an ace or a court card, the next player has to pay the correct number of cards. This continues until payment is complete without aces or court cards. Then the last player who turned up a court card or ace takes the whole pile and adds it under their own. They then start the next round with the next card in their pile.

WINNING THE GAME
The winner is the player who first goes out by using up all their cards. If nobody has gone out at the end of the time limit, the winner is the player with fewest cards.

Payments

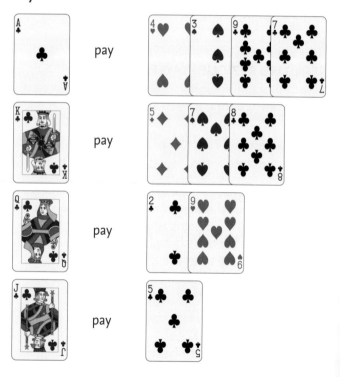

A♣   pay   4♥ 3♠ 9♣ 7♣

K♣   pay   5♦ 7♠ 8♣

Q♣   pay   2♣ 9♥

J♣   pay   5♣

Bezique

The history of bezique goes back 350 years, the standard game emerging from France. A derivation is pinochle, popular in the USA.

STANDARD BEZIQUE PLAYERS

Standard bezique is for two players, but variations exist for three or four players.

CARDS

Bezique is played with a 64-card double piquet deck – i.e. all cards below 7, except the ace, are removed from two standard 52-card decks.

One suit of a piquet deck

The ranking is ace (high), 10, K, Q, J, 9, 8, 7 (low).

AIM
Players try to gain the highest points total by making high-scoring tricks and declared melds.

PREPARING
Pencil and paper are essential for scoring unless special bezique markers or a cribbage board are available.

Players agree whether the winning score shall be 1000 points or 2000 points.

DEALING
The dealer is chosen by the higher cut. Packets of three, two and three cards are dealt in three rounds to each player, making a hand of eight cards.

The next card is placed face up to assign trumps. If this upcard is a 7, the dealer scores 10 points. A stock is made by placing all other cards face down.

PLAYING: STAGE ONE

The non-dealer leads by placing one card face up on the table. The dealer then completes the trick by adding any one of their cards.

The trick is claimed by the player who has placed the higher ranking card of the leading suit or a trump card. In the first stage, players do not have to follow suit and can use any trumps they hold.

If both people play the same card, the leading card wins the trick.

The winner of each trick may make one declaration, laying their declared meld face up on the table. The cards in a meld can also be used to make future tricks, as if they were still in the hand.

Melds and their points values are as follows:

a Double bezique (500): two Qs of spades and two Js of diamonds.
b Sequence (250): ace, 10, K, Q and J of trumps.
c Any four aces (100).
d Any four Ks (80).
e Any four Qs (60).
f Any four Js (40).
g Bezique (40): Q of spades and J of diamonds
h Royal marriage (40): a K and Q of trumps.
i Common marriage (20): a K and Q of the same non-trump suit.
j Exchange (10): changing the up-card for the 7 of trumps. Whoever holds the other 7 of trumps gains 10 points when they play it but it is not a declaration.

Cards in melds may be used for later declarations providing they are not used in similar melds. For example, an ace already used in a four aces declaration cannot be used in a second meld of four aces.

Declarations when clubs are trumps

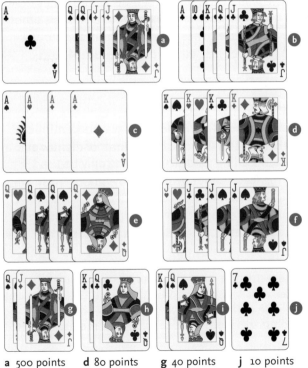

a 500 points	**d** 80 points	**g** 40 points	**j** 10 points
b 250 points	**e** 60 points	**h** 40 points	
c 100 points	**f** 40 points	**i** 20 points	

29

Scores should be recorded as the game proceeds. After the winner has made their declaration they draw cards from the stock to replace those used. The other player then replenishes their hand from the stock. When the stock is used up, players proceed to stage two.

PLAYING: STAGE TWO
The last winner of a trick leads as players continue to make eight final tricks. Now they must follow suit with each leading card. Trumps may only be used when the lead cannot be followed. A player must win the trick if possible. Play continues until players have used up their cards. The player winning the last trick gains 10 points.

When the game is complete, players gain 10 points for every brisque – i.e. an ace or a 10 contained in a trick.

Brisques

PENALTIES

1. Opponent scores 10 when a player draws out of turn.
2. Opponent scores 100 when a player holds more than eight cards.
3. A player forfeits 10 of their own points to their opponent when they play to a trick after they have failed to draw a card during the first stage of play.
4. A player forfeits all eight tricks to their opponent in stage two if they fail to follow suit or take a trick.

WINNING THE MATCH

The player to first reach 1000 or 2000 points, as agreed, is the winner.

Brag

Brag is a British game and one of the ancestors of modern poker. The game was certainly well known in England in the late 18th century and was probably played long before then. The form described here is known as three-card brag. It is the oldest and still the most popular version today.

CARDS
One standard 52-card deck. Ace is high, but may also rank as the lowest card for the purpose of making sequences.

AIM
Players try to win a 'pot' of counters by having the highest-ranking hand or by being the last player to drop out of the betting.

PREPARING
You will need a number of counters, tokens or matchsticks to use to make bets. Each player receives the same number of these at the start of the game. Before play begins, players must agree on:

- The ante: the amount that every player must contribute to the central pot before each deal (this may be nothing).

- The minimum and maximum initial bet: the amount that the first player must place in the pot in order to stay in the deal (for example, a minimum of two counters and a maximum of five).

- The betting limit: the maximum amount that the bet can be increased by subsequent players (for example, six counters).

DEALING

The first dealer is chosen at random, or by mutual consent, and the dealership subsequently passes in a clockwise direction. Before the first deal is made, the cards are shuffled by the dealer. Cards are not normally shuffled before subsequent deals in the session. Before each deal, every player must place their ante in the pot. Each player, including the dealer, receives three cards dealt face-down one at a time. Players may look at their cards immediately, or may choose to play 'blind', in which case they may not examine their cards until later in the deal.

BETTING

Betting begins with the player on the dealer's left and proceeds in a clockwise direction. The first player may 'fold' or make a bet of any number of counters between the agreed minimum and maximum. A player who folds discards their hand and takes no further part in the deal. Their cards must remain face-down on the table. If the first player folds, the next player has the same options as the first player had. If all the players fold, the last player automatically takes the contents of the pot. If the first player bets, the next player may fold or make a bet that is equal to or greater than the first player's bet. Each subsequent player must do the same in relation to the previous player.

Betting continues around the table until there are only two players who have not folded. At this point, the next player has the additional option of 'seeing' their opponent's hand. To see an opponent's hand, a player must place twice the last bet played in the pot. The opponent must then turn their cards face-up on the table. If the opponent's hand is of an equal or higher ranking than the hand belonging

to the player who paid to see it, the opponent wins
the pot and the player who paid does not expose their
cards. If the opponent's hand is of a lower ranking,
the player who paid to see it exposes their cards and
wins the pot. Hands are ranked as shown in this table:

CARD VALUES

Hand	Examples	
Prial	3♣ 3♦ 3♠ A♠ A♥ A♣ 2♦ 2♠ 2♥	'Prial' is an abbreviation of 'pair royal'. A prial hand is a hand in which all three cards are the same rank. The highest-ranking prial is a hand of threes, next is a hand of Aces and then hands of Kings, Queens, Jacks, tens, nines, eights, sevens, sixes, fives, fours and twos (lowest).
Running flush	A♠ 2♠ 3♠ A♥ K♥ Q♥ 2♣ 3♣ 4♣	A sequence of three consecutively-ranked cards from the same suit, also known as an 'on a bike' run. Ace, two and three is the highest-ranking running flush; Ace, King and Queen is next; then King, Queen and Jack and so on down to two, three and four.

Run	A♠ 2♥ 3♣	A sequence of three consecutively
	A♥ K♣ Q♠	ranked cards from different
	2♥ 3♦ 4♣	suits. Ace, two and three is the
		highest-ranking run; Ace, King
		and Queen is next; then King,
		Queen and Jack and so on
		down to two, three and four.
Flush	A♥ K♥ J♥	A set of three cards from the
	2♦ 3♦ 5♦	same suit that are not
		consecutive. Flushes are ranked
		against each other by comparing
		the highest card they contain
		first, to see which hand has the
		highest, then the middle card
		and finally the third card.
Pair	A♠ A♣ K♥	A hand that contains two cards
	2♣ 2♦ 3♠	of the same rank and a third
		card of a different rank. Pairs
		are ranked against each other by
		comparing the rank of the pair
		first, to see which hand has the
		highest and then the rank of
		the third card.

Hands are ranked in the order shown here, with prials the highest and pairs the lowest.

Hands which do not contain any of the combinations shown in the table are ranked according to the individual cards they contain. The highest cards are compared first. If they are of equal rank, the next highest cards are compared and if they too are of equal rank, the last cards are compared. When comparing by this method, and for all of the combinations shown, it is possible for hands to be equal in rank.

Betting continues until there is only one player who has not folded, or until one player pays to see their last remaining opponent's cards.

EXAMPLE OF PLAY

Example of betting in a game with five players:

Round	Player A	Player B	Player C	Player D	Player E
1	1	1	1	FOLD	2
2	2	2	2		4
3	4	FOLD	4		5
4	5		FOLD		10
5	10				10
6	20				
	(TO SEE)				

PLAYING BLIND

A player may choose to play blind once they have been dealt their cards. A player who is playing blind takes part in the betting in the same way as other players, but their bets are regarded as doubled. This means that a player only has to bet a minimum of half the last bet made. A player playing blind may choose to look at their cards at any time, but after they have done so their bets cease to be regarded as double.

If there are only two players left and one or both of them are playing blind, the option to see an opponent's hand is subject to special rules. A player who is not playing blind (an 'open' player) may not see the cards of a player who is playing blind. An open player's only options in this situation are to continue betting in the normal way or to fold. If both players are playing blind, either one may pay to see the other's cards by paying twice the minimum bet for a blind player. This would be the same as the minimum bet for an open player in the same situation. A blind player may pay to see an open player's cards by paying twice the minimum bet for a blind player.

EXAMPLE OF PLAY

Example of betting in a game with five players, two of whom are playing blind:

Round	Player A (OPEN)	Player B (BLIND)	Player C (OPEN)	Player D (BLIND)	Player E (OPEN)
1	2	1	2	1	2
2	2	1	4	2	FOLD
3	4	4	8	FOLD	
4	FOLD	4	8		
5		8			
		(TO SEE)			

1 Player A opens with a bet of two counters. Player B (playing blind) has to bet one counter to stay in the game (half of the bet required for an open player). Player C stays in the game by making the required two-counter bet. Player D (playing blind) also makes the minimum bet, as does player E.

2 Player A makes the minimum bet, as does player B. Player C increases their bet to four counters. The minimum bid for player D is now two counters, which they make. Player E folds.

3 Player A makes the minimum bet of four counters. Player B raises their bet to four counters, open players must now bet eight counters to stay in the game. Player C makes the minimum bet of eight counters. Player D folds.

4 Player A folds. Player B now has the option of seeing player C's cards, but decides to make the minimum bet of four counters instead. Player C may not pay to see player B's cards because an open player may not pay to see a blind player's cards. Player C makes the minimum bet of eight counters.

5 Player B exercises their option to see their open opponent's cards by paying eight counters. Betting ends.

If all the players fold apart from a blind player, the blind player retains their hand and a second hand is dealt to them in the usual way in the next deal. That player must then choose whether to examine the hand from the previous deal, examine the new hand or examine neither hand. They may not examine both hands. If a player chooses to look at one of the hands, they may choose to keep that hand and discard the other, in which case they are no longer blind, or discard that hand and keep the other. If they discard the hand they have looked at they may continue playing blind with the other hand, or look at it and continue as an open player.

If a player decides not to look at either hand, they play the next deal with two blind hands. They may choose to look at either one of their hands during the course of the next deal and revert to open play, or they may look at neither and continue to play blind. A player who wins a deal with two blind hands must discard one of them, unexamined, before the next deal.

All folded cards are collected unexamined, and placed at the bottom of the deck before the next deal takes place. The winner's cards are also collected and placed at the bottom of the deck. If the winner's hand was blind, no player may examine the cards. If the winner's hand was open and was not seen, no player may examine the cards. In these cases, the cards are not shuffled before the next deal. If the winner's hand was seen or if the winner's hand was seen and their last opponent's hand was revealed, the cards are shuffled before the next deal.

Canasta

Canasta originated in Uruguay around 1940 and quickly spread to the rest of South, and then North, America. The rules for canasta were standardised in the United States in the 1950s. The game became extremely popular and, for a time, seemed set to supplant contract bridge as the world's favourite.

AIM
To win the largest number of points by melding all the cards in your hand with your partner's cards before the opposition.

CARDS
Canasta is played with 108 cards, so two standard 52-card decks and four jokers are required.

Card	Points
Joker	50
Ace and 2	20
K, Q, J, 10, 9, 8	10
7, 6, 5, 4	5

Point values for cards

The cards Ace, King, Queen, Jack, ten, nine, eight, seven, six, five and four are known as the natural cards. Twos and Jokers are wild cards and may be substituted for any natural card in most instances. Threes have special functions and point values explained later.

PARTNERSHIPS AND DEALING

Partnerships are decided randomly or by mutual consent, as is the first dealer. The deal passes clockwise to the next player on the left at the end of each hand.

The player to the left of the dealer shuffles the cards, and the player to the right shuffles them before the deal is made. Each player receives eleven cards dealt face-down and one at a time.

The rest of the cards are placed face-down in the centre of the table as the 'stock'.

The top card of the stock is placed, face-up, next to the stock to start the discard pile. The top card of the discard pile must be a natural card at this stage of the game. If the first card is a wild card, or a red three (heart or diamond), another card from the stock must be placed on top of it.

Players must immediately place any red threes they have been dealt face-up on the table in front of them and replace them with an equal number of cards from the stock.

MELDS
Achieving melds is the main element of play in canasta. There are several rules that restrict the formation of melds.

A meld consists of three or more cards with the same face value. Every meld must contain at least two natural cards. The smallest melds must, therefore, consist of three natural cards of the same face value, or two natural cards of the same face value and a wild card. A meld may not contain more than three wild cards.

A meld of seven cards is known as a canasta. Since no meld may contain more than three wild cards, a canasta will always contain at least four natural cards. A partnership must achieve at least one canasta before a member of that partnership can legally get rid of all of their cards and end the game. There is no legal limit to the size of a meld, but it may never contain more than three wild cards. Logically, since there are only eight cards of any one face value in the deck, the largest possible meld would contain eleven cards.

A meld with no wild cards is known as 'natural', a meld with wild cards is known as a 'mixed meld'. The same terms apply to canastas.

PLAYING

Play begins with the player to the left of the dealer and passes in a clockwise direction. Partners should sit so that play alternates between one team and the other.

To start their turn a player must pick up the top card from the stock. Alternatively, they may, under certain conditions, pick the entire discard pile up. The player may then meld, if they have the opportunity. Melding is not compulsory.

To end a turn, a player must discard one card face-up on the discard pile. A player may not discard their last card if their partnership has not made a canasta. To avoid this, a player must play in such a way that they are able to discard at the end of their turn while still retaining at least one card. A player cannot avoid discarding.

A player may pick up the entire discard pile if they are able to use the top card of the pile with at least two other cards from their hand (natural or wild) to form a meld.

To pick up the discard pile, a player places the two or more cards from their hand that will be used in the meld face-up on the table. They add the top card from the discard pile to form the meld and add the rest of the discard pile to their hand. They may then form further melds before finally discarding a card to end their turn.

Freezing

The discard pile is not always available to a partnership. It may be 'frozen' (not available) under three circumstances:

- The discard pile is frozen to all players if it contains a wild card. When a wild card is placed on the discard pile, it is positioned at 90 degrees to the other cards so that it remains visible after subsequent discards have been placed on top of it.
- The discard pile is frozen to all players if the first card from the stock was a red three. A red three is positioned in the same way as a wild card so that it remains visible.
- The discard pile is frozen to a partnership until it makes its first meld.

A player may only take the discard pile when it is frozen if they can form a meld with the top card and at least two natural cards (not wild cards) from their hand.

Meld requirements
A partnership may only lay down its first meld if it has a minimum point value. This value depends on the partnership's cumulative score from previous hands.

The initial meld requirements may be met by laying down more than one meld at once.

The discard pile is frozen before a partnership's initial meld, so the first meld must come from the hand plus whatever is drawn from the stock, or the requirements for taking the frozen discard pile must be met. When making an initial meld from the discard pile, only the top card of the pile counts towards the point value of that meld.

Any red threes that a player may have put down before making an initial meld do not count towards the initial meld score. Even a full canasta may not be put down if it does not meet the score required. The only exception to the initial meld requirements is when a player, having drawn from the stock, is able to meld all of their cards, including a canasta, with or without making a discard.

Threes

The following rules apply to red threes:

- A player dealt a red three must immediately place it face-up on the table and draw a replacement card from the stock. Bonuses are awarded at the end of a deal for these threes.
- If a red three is turned up as the first card of the discard pile it is turned 90 degrees so that it remains visible and another card from the stock is placed on top of it. The player who takes a discard pile frozen in this way immediately places the red three face-up on the table, but does not draw a replacement for it.

The following rules apply to black threes:

- Discarding a black three prevents the next player from taking the discard pile. This effect only lasts until a subsequent card is discarded on top of the black three (at the end of the next player's turn).
- Black threes may not be melded unless a player is going out. In this case a player may meld three or four black threes but black-three melds must not include wild cards.

Ending play

- A player who legally gets rid of all their cards is said to have 'gone out'.
- A deal ends when the first player goes out.
- A player who goes out by laying down their entire hand, including a canasta, without having previously made any melds is said to have 'gone out concealed', which earns a points bonus.
- A player can only go out if their partnership has achieved at least one canasta. Forming the canasta may be part of a player's last turn.
- After drawing from the stock, but before going out, a player has the option of asking their partner 'may I go out?'. They must then comply with their partner's answer of 'yes' or 'no'. It is not compulsory to ask a partner's permission to go out.
- A deal also ends if there are no more cards left in the stock at the point where a player is required to draw one.

SCORING

As soon as play has ended, each partnership scores its hand. This score consists of:

- The total value of all of the cards they have melded (see Point values for cards, page 44).
- Minus the total value of any cards remaining in the hand.
- Plus the total of any bonuses (see Bonus points below).

Cumulative point scores are kept for both partnerships. The first side to win 5000 points wins the game.

BONUS POINTS

Going out	100
Going out concealed (in addition to going out bonus)	100
Each natural canasta	500
Each mixed canasta	300
Each red three* (if team has at least one meld)	100
All red threes** (in addition to individual red three bonuses)	400

*Red threes score -100 points if no meld
**All red threes score -400 if no meld

STRATEGY TIPS

- It is rarely an advantage to go out as quickly as possible. The more cards you can collect in your hand, the more opportunities you have for forming canastas and the more points you will have the opportunity to win.
- It is almost always a good idea to take a large discard pile if you are able. It gives you many more cards to form melds with and denies their use to the opposition.
- Small discard piles are rarely worth taking because the opposition will remember most of the cards in the pile and know what you have.
- Do not meld wild cards if you have the corresponding natural cards. Always save wild cards as long as possible.
- You do not have to meld everything in your hand. For example, if you have five kings, you can meld three of them and keep the other two hidden in your hand in case you need them later to take a frozen discard pile.

- Black threes are valuable cards because they can always be discarded without the risk of giving the opposition a card they need.
- If your opponents secure control of a large discard pile try to go out as quickly as you can in order to minimise the points they can gain.

Card dominoes

A game of skill and chance for two or more players, also known as sevens, fan-tan or parliament.

AIM
Each person tries to be the first to add their cards in sequence to a layout on the table.

DEALING
All 52 cards in a standard deck are dealt one at a time, face down, to each player in clockwise order.

PLAYING
Players sort their own cards into sequences in each suit. Whoever holds the 7 of diamonds begins play by putting it face up on the table. In turn, clockwise, players add a diamond card in sequence:

a going up from 7 through 8, 9, 10, J, Q, K; or
b going down from 7 through 6, 5, 4, 3, 2, ace.

A player can add a card to a sequence or start a new sequence with another 7. If they cannot do either, they pass and the turn goes to the next player.

WINNING THE GAME

The first player to use up all their cards is the winner but the game goes on until everyone has played their cards and completed the four sequences.

Example of play in progress

Casino

Originating in 15th-century France, this gambling game, while relatively easy to learn, requires skill with numbers.

PLAYERS
Two, three or four people can play.

CARDS
The standard deck of 52 cards is used, the ace ranking low at a face value of 1. All other cards count at face value. Court cards have no numerical denomination.

AIM
Individuals score by capturing certain cards.

DEALING
The player making the lowest cut becomes the dealer.

Two players: the non-dealer gets two cards face down, two cards are placed face up on the table and two are dealt face down to the dealer. This is repeated until both players have a hand of four cards and four are face up on the table.

Three or four players: two cards are dealt face down to every player, including the dealer, then two face up on the table. This process is repeated once more.

PLAYING

The player to the dealer's left begins by playing at least one card to 'capture', 'build' or 'trail' cards. The others then play in turn by clockwise rotation.

FOUR WAYS OF CAPTURING CARDS

a   A pair can be made by capturing a face-up card with the same numerical value as a card in the hand. The player puts their card face down on the captured card and pulls the cards towards them.

Two or more face-up cards can be captured if a player holds a card to match each of them in value.

b   A group can be made by capturing two or more cards totalling the numerical value of a card in the hand.

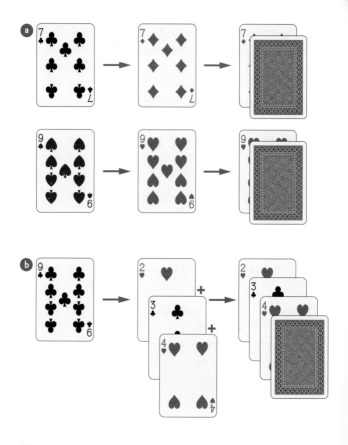

c A group and a pair can be made by capturing a group of two or three cards with the same value as one of the player's cards as well as a single card with the same value. A sweep is the capture of all four face-up cards in one turn.

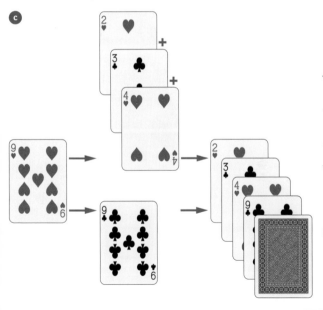

d Court cards can be captured by making a pair or a group of all four, providing a matching court card is held. A group cannot be made with only three court cards.

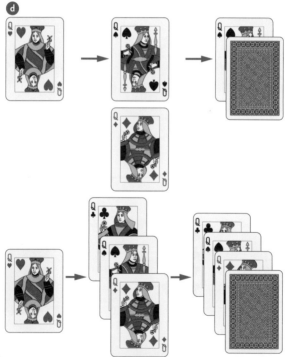

TWO WAYS OF BUILDING

Face-up cards can be built on by adding cards from the hand. The purpose of building is to make it possible to capture cards. Court cards cannot be used in builds.

1 A player can make a single build by placing a card from their hand face up onto one of the face-up cards if:

   a the total value of the cards is not greater than 10; and

   b they hold, and declare, a card equal in value to their single build. For example, a player holding a 7 and a 4 may build the 4 on a face up 3 and declare 'building 7' (page 64).

Subsequently another player holding an ace and an 8 may, in turn, build the ace onto the 3+4 and declare 'building 8'. Cards being built remain in the centre of the table.

2) A player may also change an existing single build into a multiple build. This is done by increasing the value of an existing single build and then using other cards to add another build of the same value, placing it at the side of the first build.

Building 7

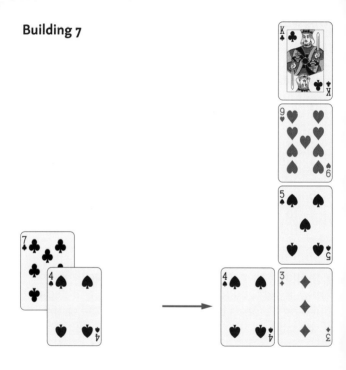

Building 8

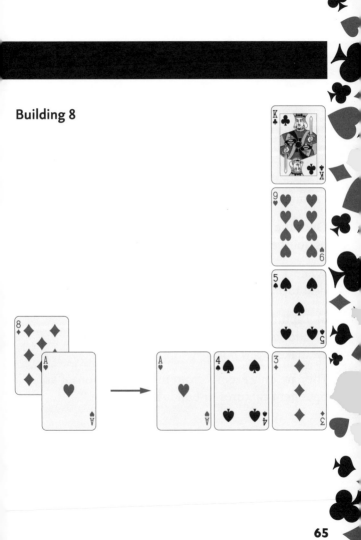

For example, a multiple build of 9 (see page 67) could be made on an existing single build of 5 by a player who holds a 4, plus 4, 5 and 9. They would declare 'building 9s'. Their aim is use the 9 to capture all the cards in their next turn, hoping that nobody else captures it first.

Once the value of a multiple build has been established it cannot be changed.

When a player has made or added to a build, in their next turn they must:

a) capture the build; or
b) add to a build; or
c) make a new build.

They are only exempt from these obligations if an opponent captures or builds before them.

TRAILING
A player who cannot capture or build then trails by adding one card from their hand to the face-up cards on the table.

A multiple build of 9

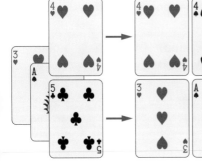

RENEWING THE HAND

When all players have no cards left they are dealt another four cards each in packets of two, but no more are dealt to the centre of the table. New face-up cards can only come from a player who trails.

COMPLETING A ROUND

When the pack runs out, any cards remaining face up are claimed by the player who made the last capture.

For each new round, players take the deal in turn. Six rounds complete a game.

SCORING

Only captured cards score points, as follows:

2 of spades (little casino)	1 point
10 of diamonds (big casino)	2 points
Each ace	1 point
Seven or more spades	1 point
27 or more cards	3 points
A sweep	1 point

WINNING THE GAME
The winner is the player who gets the highest score over six rounds or the first player to reach 21 points.

Clock is a fast-paced and intriguing patience game that owes much of its popularity to the unusual nature of its layout. The chances of getting all the cards out are small, which is probably another reason why players come back to it again and again. The same game is sometimes known as Sundial or Travellers.

AIM
To organise thirteen piles of cards laid out in the position of numbers on a clock face, so that all the Aces are at the one o'clock position, all twos at two o'clock and so on, with the Queens at the twelve o'clock position and the Kings at the centre.

CARDS
Clock is played with a single standard deck of 52 cards. The cards in their suits rank with Kings highest, followed by Queens, Jacks, tens, nines, eights, sevens, sixes, fives, fours, threes, twos and Aces (lowest).

DEALING
The cards are dealt, one at a time and face-down, to

form twelve piles of four cards in the position of the numbers on a clock face with a thirteenth pile in the centre of the circle. Four cards may be dealt to each pile before moving on to the next, or each pile can be built up one card at a time.

PLAYING

The top card of the centre pile is turned over and placed next to the appropriate pile in the circle. For example, if the first card turned over is an eight, it is placed next to the pile in the eight o'clock position. If the first card is a Jack, it is placed next to the pile in the eleven o'clock position.

The top card from the pile that the last card was placed next to is turned over and placed next to the appropriate pile in the circle. The same thing is done with the top card of that pile and so on.

A card may be placed next to the pile that it came from. For example, if the top card from the pile in the eight o'clock position is turned over and it is an eight, that card is placed next to the pile it came from and another card from the same pile is turned over.

Kings are placed next to the central pile and a card from that pile is turned over and placed next to the appropriate pile.

If there are no more cards left in a pile, the card from the next pile in sequence is turned over and allocated. For example, if an eight is turned over and there are no more cards left in the pile at the eight o'clock position, a card is turned over from the pile in the nine o'clock position, or the next pile in clockwise sequence that still has cards. This will always happen when the fourth card of a particular rank is found.

The game ends when the fourth King is turned up. If the fourth King is not the last card to be turned up, the game is lost because there is no pile next in sequence from which a card can be taken to continue the game, and no further moves may be made.

Cribbage

Thought to have been developed by Sir John Suckling, a poet and member of the English court in the early 17th century, cribbage requires a quick mind.

PLAYERS
The most popular game is six-card cribbage for two players. There are variations for three or four players as well.

CARDS
A standard 52-card deck is used, all cards having their face value (ace is 1) and court cards counting 10.

THE CRIBBAGE BOARD
Although pencil and paper can be used for scoring, a cribbage board is much simpler. Usually a block of wood 10in by 3in, the board has four rows of 30 holes, in six groups of five pairs, two rows per player. At each end of the board are one or two game holes where the players keep their scoring pegs.

MOVING THE PEGS TO SCORE

Each player uses two pegs, moving them alternately, first along the outer row and then along the inner.

a The first score is marked by moving a peg the same number of holes along the outer row of holes.

b The second score is marked by using a second peg to mark out the same number of holes beyond the first peg.

c The third score is marked by using the first peg to count that score beyond the second peg.

d To mark the next score, the peg that is behind is used to mark the score onwards from the front peg. Scoring continues until the front peg reaches the game hole by passing the end of the inner row.

(for two players)

AIM
The first player to go twice round the board, getting 121 points, wins the game.

DEALING
Players cut the deck and the one with the lower cut is first dealer. The dealer deals six cards, face down and one at a time, to each player, beginning with their opponent. The rest of the deck is put aside.

THE CRIB
Each player then discards two cards and places them face down to the right of the dealer to form the crib. The dealer will claim it as part of their score.

THE CUT
After the crib has been made, the non-dealer cuts the remaining deck. The top card is turned over by the dealer and left face up on the pack to be the start or starter. If this card is a J, two points 'for his heels' are scored by the dealer.

SCORING

Points can be scored for groups of cards made during play and when the hand is shown at the end. The following groups of cards score points:

a	Pair (two cards of the same rank)	2 points
b	Pair royal (three of the same rank)	6 points
c	Double pair royal (all four cards of the same rank)	12 points
d	Run (a sequence of cards in rank order)	1 point per card of any suit
e	Flush (any four or five cards of the same suit). If also a run, it scores for both flush and run.	1 point per card
f	Fifteen (any group of cards with a total face value of 15)	2 points

Scoring

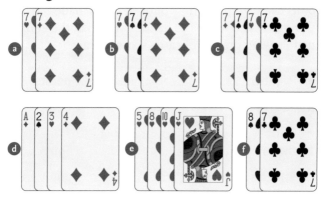

PLAYING

The non-dealer places one card from their hand face up in front of them and calls out its numerical value. The dealer then does the same.

The players continue to call as they add a card to their own spread of cards in turn, scoring for a pair, pair royal, run or fifteen they make with their opponent's card during play. Flushes are not taken into account during play.

Examples of some calls

Player	Card	Call	Score
Non-dealer	ace	'one'	0
Dealer	2	'run for two' (ace, 2)	2
Non-dealer	4	'four'	0
Dealer	5	'run for two'	2
Non-dealer	3	'fifteen for seven'	7

The non-dealer makes seven points from a fifteen: 1+2+4+5+3=15 (two points plus a run: ace, 2, 4, 5, 3 (five points). Cards in a run do not have to have been played in the correct order.

THE COUNT

The face value of the cards is totalled as play proceeds. A sample count is shown for six cards played alternately by non-dealer and dealer.

Sample count	
Ace clubs	1
Ace hearts	1
4 spades	4
5 clubs	5
10 diamonds	10
J clubs	10

The face values add up to 31, the limit for the count. The player whose card reaches a count of 31 scores two extra points and both players' face-up cards are turned face down.

A player who cannot keep the count within 31 at their turn must call 'go'.

The opponent then plays any card low enough to keep the total below 31. If the count then reaches 31, they get two points; if it is still less than 31, they get one point and call 'go'.

Play begins again, but with only the cards remaining in the hands, and continues until the count reaches 31 or all cards have been played. The player of the last card of a hand gains 'one for the last'.

THE SHOW

When all four cards of the hand have been played, the non-dealer begins the show by picking up their cards and showing the scores they can make with them.

If the non-dealer is close to reaching the winning score of 121, being the first to show can be an advantage.

They then organise their cards in any combination for scoring (see Scoring **a** to **f** on page 77). Both players can include the start card in their show. For example, if the start card is 4 hearts and a player has 4 clubs, 5 hearts, 6 clubs and 6 spades, the scoring combinations of 4, 4, 5, 6, 6 are:

8 points for fifteen (four combinations of 4, 5, 6);

12 points for runs (four runs of 4, 5, 6); and

4 points for pairs (5, 5, and 6, 6); making a total of 24 points.

Sample show of 24 points

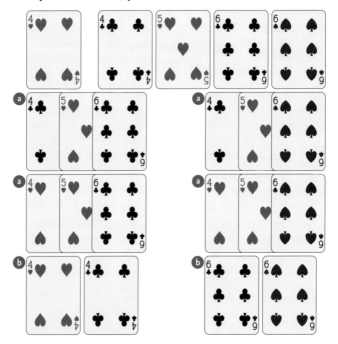

Scoring combinations
a   8 points for fifteen and 12 points for runs
b   4 points for pairs

SCORING CARDS OF THE SAME SUIT

A player holding a J of the same suit as the start card scores 'one for his nob'.

A player holding a flush of four cards of the same suit scores four points, but a four-card flush cannot be made with the start card. However, the start card can be added to make a flush of five, scoring five points.

When the non-dealer has finished scoring their cards, the dealer does the same with first their own cards and then with the cards in the crib. The crib is scored like a hand, but only a five-card flush is counted. The dealer adds the crib score to their own.

Five-card flush in hearts

start card   cards in hand

CONVENTIONS

A redeal is required if there are errors in dealing. If a dealing mistake is found after play has begun, the non-dealer gains two points and the cards are redealt or extra cards are drawn from the stock pile.

If a player does not play their extra cards after a call of 'go', they may not play those cards later and their opponent gains two points. There are no penalties for counting errors during play.

A player scores an extra game in their favour if they reach a score of 121 before their opponent is halfway round the board – i.e. before they reach 61. This is called a 'lurch'. In a rule not always used, a player may call their opponent 'muggins' when they have missed a score they could have made. The player can then add the missed score to their own.

Ecarté

Meaning 'discarded', ecarté was popular in 19th-century France. Derivations of the game are the USA version called euchre and the three-handed game of five-hundred.

PLAYERS
Two people play against each other.

CARDS
All cards below 7 are removed from a standard 52-card deck to make a deck of 32. The rank from high to low is K, Q, J, A, 10, 9, 8, 7. Two cards make a trick.

Rank

high   low

AIM
To score points by making tricks.

PREPARING
Paper and pencil are needed for keeping the scores. Using the ranking of the 32-card deck, players cut for seat position, first deal and choice of deal for the whole game.

DEALING
The first dealer shuffles the cards and invites the non-dealer to cut. They deal five cards face down to their opponent and to themselves, in packets of three then two or in packets of two then three.

The dealer places the eleventh card face up on the table to assign trumps. If it is a K, the dealer gains one point.

The remaining cards are piled face down to form a stock. If the non-dealer holds the king of trumps, they can gain a point if they choose to declare it.

The deal

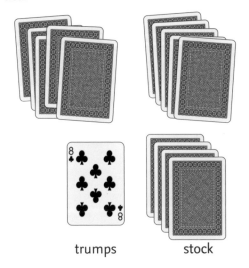

trumps   stock

THE EXCHANGE

An exchange of cards can take place before play commences but only if the non-dealer proposes one and the dealer accepts.

To exchange, the non-dealer discards cards face down, which are then dead, and takes the same number of replacement cards from the stock. The dealer can then make an exchange. This process continues until stopped by the dealer declaring 'play' or until the stock pile runs out, when play must start. An exchange cannot be proposed by the dealer but they can continue to exchange after the non-dealer signals they do not wish to exchange by calling 'I play'.

An exchange should not be proposed or accepted if a player holds cards with which at least three tricks could be made.

PLAYING
The non-dealer leads with one card face up. The dealer must play a card of the same suit if they hold one. If not, their next option is a trump card; failing both, they can play any other card.

Tricks are won by the card of the leading suit that is higher in rank or by a trump card.

If trumps are led, only a higher ranking trump wins the trick. The player winning a trick leads the next and so on until all five tricks are complete.

SCORING

There are four ways of gaining points:

a Three tricks gains one point.

b Five tricks, called a 'vole', gains two points.

c King of trumps gains one point for the dealer if turned up immediately after the deal (see Dealing) or for a player who holds it if they declared it before playing their first card.

d One point is gained if an opponent fails to make three tricks after refusing an exchange. Five points wins the game.

Euchre

Originally one of the most popular trump games in the USA, euchre, which derives from ecarté, probably arrived in Louisiana with the French settlers.

PLAYERS
Four people play in pairs, partners sitting opposite each other.

CARDS
Every card below 7 is removed from a standard deck of 52 cards to make a 32-card deck in which ace ranks high unless the suit is trumps.

In a trump suit the J from the suit of the same colour is included and the ranking order from high to low is J trumps, J suit of same colour, A trumps, K trumps, Q trumps, 10, 9, 8 and 7 trumps.

Rank order when clubs is an ordinary suit

Rank order when clubs is trumps

AIM
Partners cooperate to win tricks.

PREPARING
Each partnership takes the 3 and 4 of one suit from the stripped cards to use as score cards.

The lowest cut of the deck decides who deals. The dealer shuffles and offers the cut to the player on their left.

The players should agree at this stage whether they are going to play for a five-, seven- or ten-point game.

DEALING

Beginning on the dealer's left, cards are dealt face down in packets of three cards to each player on the first round and packets of two on the second round.

The next card, known as the upcard, is placed face up on the table to assign trumps. The remainder are placed faced down to form a stock.

BIDDING FOR TRUMPS

Starting with the player to the dealer's left, every player can bid to accept or reject the upcard as trumps.

In the first round, the dealer's opponents can accept by saying 'I order it up', their partner by saying 'I assist' and the dealer can accept by discarding one card from their hand and replacing it with the upcard.

If one player accepts the upcard, play begins.

Alternatively, the upcard can be rejected by non-dealers saying 'I pass' and by the dealer placing the card face up and visible under the stock.

If all players reject the upcard, a second round of bidding allows each player to either pass or nominate a different suit as trumps. The first nomination becomes the trump suit, and play begins.

If all players pass in the second round, cards are shuffled and redealt by the next player in turn clockwise.

The player who accepted the trump suit in the first round or who nominated it in the second can choose to play solo by declaring 'I play alone'.

Their partner places their cards face down and takes no further part in that round, although it is still the partnership that scores points.

PLAYING
The player to the left of the dealer leads with one card face up. Players must then play cards of the same suit. If they cannot follow suit, they play either a trump card or any other suit.

The player of the highest ranking card wins the trick and leads for the next trick.

SCORING
The following points can be gained:

a March (all five tricks): 2 points
b March for a solo player: 4 points
c Three or four tricks: 1 point
d Euchred opponents – i.e. if they have made fewer than three tricks: 2 points

The partners keep their scores by using the two cards from the stripped pack as follows:

a 1 point: place the 3 with the other across it
b 2 points: place the 4 with the other across it
c 3 points: place the 3 on top of the other card
d 4 points: place the 4 on top of the other card

Scoring for higher scores is best done on paper.

Keeping the scores

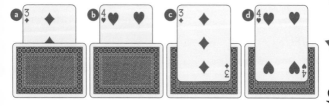

WINNING THE GAME

Five, seven or ten points wins the game, as agreed at the start

A game of chance and skill for two, but better with more players. A standard deck of cards is used. A happy families pack may be preferred by younger players.

AIM
Players try to get rid of all their cards.

DEALING
If two or three are playing, each is dealt seven cards; if four or five, each gets five cards. The remaining cards are placed face down to form the stock, or fish pile.

PLAYING
Players sort their own cards into groups of the same rank (number or picture), keeping them hidden from the others. The person on the left of the dealer asks anyone for cards of the same rank as one they hold. For example, if they hold the 6 of hearts in their hand they might say, 'John, give me your 6s.' If 'John' has any, he must give them to the asker. The asker can

then ask someone else for cards either of the same rank as the first or a different rank, as long as they hold one such card in their hand. They can go on asking for cards until a player does not have the card they want.

A player who does not have a card of the requested rank tells the asker to 'fish'. The person told to fish takes one card from the fish pile, and the person who said 'fish' continues the game by becoming the asker.

Anyone who collects all four cards in a set puts the cards face down in front of them.

WINNING THE GAME
The winner is the first person to have no cards left except a collection of sets. If two people run out of cards together, the one with the most sets wins.

Sets are four cards of the same rank

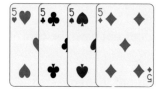 

Five hundred

A member of the euchre family, five hundred shares similarities with whist and bridge.

PLAYERS
The basic game is for three players; it can be played by two or four players, as well.

CARDS
All cards below 7 are stripped from a standard 52-card deck and a joker is added to make a 33-card deck.

The rank order of the trump suit from high to low is joker, J trumps (known as right bower), J of same colour suit (left bower), ace, K, Q, 10, 9, 8 and 7 of trumps.

The rank order in no-trump hands is ace, K, Q, J, 10, 9, 8 and 7; there are no bowers. The joker becomes whatever suit is chosen by the person who holds it, and it ranks highest in that suit, taking any trick in which it is played.

A trick is a group of three cards, one played by each person in turn.

Rank order when spades are trumps

high   low

right   left
bower   bower

Rank order of all suits when there are no trumps
(Joker is nominated as clubs in this example.)

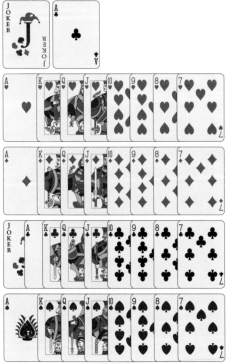

high   low

AIM

Individuals bid to make a contract and attempt to win by fulfilling it.

DEALING

The cards are cut for the deal. K ranks highest, joker lowest and ace next to lowest. The lowest cut determines the dealer.

Beginning with the player to the dealer's left, 10 cards are dealt to each player, face down in packets. The dealer can choose between: packets of three, two, three and two or packets of three, three, three and one.

The three cards left are called the widow and are placed in a pile face up on the table.

If there is any misdeal, the cards are thrown in and redealt by the next person in clockwise rotation.

BIDDING

The player on the dealer's left begins by bidding the number of tricks they expect to make and stating their choice of trumps. Players must bid to make at least six tricks and not more than 10.

Each player bids in turn, clockwise, or passes. A pass prevents the player from making any further bid in that round.

Bids are ranked, from high to low: no-trumps, hearts, diamonds, clubs, spades. It can be seen from the scoring table that the most valuable contract is '10 no trumps' – i.e. 10 tricks without any trump suit, worth 520 points. The least valuable contract is 'six spades' – i.e. six tricks with spades as trumps, worth 40 points.

The player who makes the highest bid wins the contract and takes the widow cards. They then discard face down any three cards from their hand.

PLAYING
The player winning the contract is opposed by the other two who play as a partnership, although they each score for their own tricks.

The contract winner leads by placing one card face up on the table. The others follow suit, clockwise. Anyone who cannot follow the leading suit may play a card from another suit.

The winner of the trick is the person playing:

a the highest card of the leading suit; or
b the highest trump card, if the contract was for a suit rather than for no-trumps; or
c the joker.

The player winning the trick leads to the next one.

SCORING
If the winning bidder has fulfilled the contract, they score as shown on the table. If not, they lose points to the value of the contract and their score may be a minus figure.

Scoring table for five hundred (values of contracts)

Tricks bid	♠	♣	♦	♥	No trumps
6	40	60	80	100	120
7	140	160	180	200	220
8	240	260	280	300	320
9	340	360	380	400	420
10	440	460	480	500	520

The opponents each score 10 points for each of their own tricks.

BONUS POINTS
When a player who contracted to make eight or fewer tricks makes a grand slam (takes all 10 tricks), they gain 250 points. There are no other bonus points for making more tricks than contracted.

An optional bonus for a grand slam made by a player who contracted to make eight or more tricks is to double the value of the contract.

WINNING THE GAME
A score of 500 points wins the game. If two players both reach 500 in the same deal, the one who reached it first is the winner.

Gin rummy

A simple, fast, two-handed variation of rummy. The rules are the same as for rummy except as described here.

CARDS
Two standard decks of cards are used, one being dealt while the other is being shuffled by another player in readiness for the next round. The cards rank normally with ace low.

Rank

high   low

PLAYERS
Standard gin rummy is for two players. It can be played by any number of people, by dividing the players into two sides. Pairs can then play against each other simultaneously.

AIM

Each player tries to meld all their cards, but they can still win under certain circumstances even when they do not do this.

PREPARING

Pencil and paper should be to hand for scoring. Players agree to one of the following:

a the number of rounds to be played;
b a maximum score; or
c a time limit on the match.

DEALING

The person cutting the higher card can choose which deck to use, where to sit and if they want to deal. Beginning with their opponent, they deal 10 cards each, singly and face down. The 21st card is turned up and this upcard starts the discard pile. The other cards are placed face down to form the stock pile.

PLAYING

The non-dealer can take the upcard if they want it. If not, the dealer may take it. If they do not, the non-dealer must take a card from the stock.

The players take a card in turn, and must discard one, building melds in their hands. No melds are laid on the table until one player 'goes knocking' or 'goes gin' when it is their turn, or until only two cards are left in the stock.

ENDING THE ROUND

a   Going gin happens when a player melds all 10 cards.
b   Knocking is an option when the value of unmelded cards totals 10 or less. To knock, a player draws a card at their turn, knocks on the table and throws away one card. Melds and unmelded cards are laid down. The other player then puts down their cards and can lay off any of their unmelded cards on the opponent's melds.

c A tie is declared and a new hand dealt by the same dealer when two cards remain in the stock and the last player cannot go gin or knock. No points are scored. When the round is over, a line is drawn under or around the score of the player winning that hand.

This is called a box.

SCORING POINTS
Scores for each hand and a running total are kept for each player. Points can be gained in four ways:

1 a gin gains 25 points plus the value of the loser's unmelded cards;
2 a player who knocks gets the difference in value between the unmelded cards of the two players unless their opponent has an unmelded card count equal, to or greater than theirs. Then the opponent gets the points plus a bonus of 25 points;
3 every box (winning hand) nets 25 points;
4 a bonus of 100 points is gained by the player to first reach 100 points in a game.

Sample of scoring sheet for one game

Hand	Player A	score total	Player B	score total
1st	11	11	0	0
2nd	0	11	5	5
3rd	19	30	0	5
4th	0	30	27	32
5th	25	55	0	32
6th	21	76	0	32
7th	45	121	0	32
Total		121		32
Game bonus		100		
Boxes		125		50
Total score		346		84

Give away

An easy game for two or more players who enjoy speed and alertness. A standard deck of cards is used.

AIM
Players try to be first to get rid of their cards.

DEALING
All the cards are dealt out, one at a time and face down, without anyone seeing them. The cards stay face down in a pile in front of each player. An unequal number of cards in each hand does not matter.

PLAYING
The player on the dealer's left turns their top card over.

If it is an ace, they place it in the middle of the table and turn another card over. If it is the 2 of the same suit, they add it to the ace.

When a card is neither an ace nor a card that can be added to any other face-up card, going up or down in sequence, it is placed next to the player's own pile and the turn passes to the next person clockwise.

Sequences are built in rank order ace, 2, 3, 4, 5, 6, 7, 8, 9, 10, J, Q, K. Cards can be added to the centre or to any player's pile of upturned cards.

If a player's last card goes onto their own upturn pile, they wait until their next turn to turn the pile over, face down, and start again taking from the top.

If their last card goes into the centre or onto another's pile, the player can immediately turn their pile over and continue to play.

The winner is the one who is the first to discard all their cards either onto the centre pile or another player's upturn pile.

Play to centre   Play to own or other's face-up card

Go boom

A simple game for two or more players, which very young children can also enjoy. A standard deck of cards is used in which ace ranks high.

AIM
Everyone tries to get rid of all their cards first.

DEALING
Players cut; highest cut deals seven cards, one at a time, to each player clockwise. The remaining cards are put face down in the centre of the table.

PLAYING
All players sort their cards and the person to the dealer's left starts the round by placing one of their cards face up on the table.

The next player, clockwise, adds a card that is:

a the same suit (all hearts etc.); or
b the same rank (number or picture) as the one before.

When a player cannot follow with one of the above, they pick cards from the spare pile until they get a card they can play.

When everyone has played in that round, the person who played the highest ranking card starts the next round. If there is a tie, the one who played first starts the next round. When the spare pile runs out, a player has to say 'pass' and it is the next player's turn.

WINNING THE GAME
The first to get rid of all their cards is the winner. They proclaim this by shouting 'boom'.

Hearts

A 19th-century game in which players try to avoid taking penalty cards.

PLAYERS
Any number from three to seven people, each playing for themselves.

CARDS
The standard 52-card deck is used. Ace ranks high and there are no trump cards. The 2s are stripped from the deck according to the number of players. The 2 of hearts is always retained. One card played by each person in turn makes a trick.

TABLE OF NUMBERS

players	stripped cards	cards in a trick
three	one 2	3
four	none	4
five	two 2s	5
six	three 2s	6
seven	three 2s	7

AIM

Players make tricks and score penalty points for every hearts card they win. Thus the aim is to score zero by not winning any heart cards in tricks.

PREPARING

Paper and pencil will be needed for scoring penalty points. Players should agree beforehand how the game is to be won. The options are:

1 the game ends when one person reaches a penalty score of 50 points; or
2 the game ends when an agreed number of rounds have been played, usually four or five.

DEALING

The player making the lowest cut becomes the dealer. Beginning with the player on their left, they deal the cards face down, singly, to each player in clockwise rotation, until all the cards are dealt.

NUMBER OF CARDS IN EACH HAND

players	deck	hand
three	51	17
four	52	13
five	50	10
six	49	8 (the last card put aside)
seven	49	7

PLAYING

The player on the left of the dealer leads the first trick by playing one card. The other players must follow suit if they can. If not, they may play any other card. The trick is claimed by the person playing the highest ranking card of the lead suit. That player leads the next trick. The hand ends when all 13 heart cards have been played, unless a player fails to correct a revoke.

REVOKING

If a player revokes – i.e., fails to follow suit when they could have – they may correct their mistake before the trick is claimed. Otherwise they score 13 penalty points and the round ends immediately. No penalties are scored by the other players. The deal for the next round passes clockwise to the player on the left of the last dealer.

SCORING

At the end of each round, every heart card in a player's tricks counts as one penalty point. Any cards left in the hand do not count.

Cards scoring one penalty point

WINNING THE GAME

The winner is the player with the lowest number of penalty points at the agreed stage of the game – i.e., after a player has scored 50 points or the agreed number of rounds has been played (see Preparing).

Knaves

A game for three players using a standard deck with aces high. Played like whist, but Js in tricks taken count as minus points.

Rank

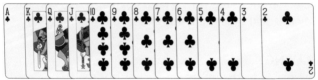

high   low

AIM
To score points for tricks taken, while avoiding penalties for tricks with Js. A trick is a group of three cards, one played by each person in turn.

PREPARING
Paper and pencil are needed for scoring.

DEALING
The player making the highest cut becomes the first dealer. The whole deck is dealt in clockwise direction,

beginning with the player on the dealer's left.

Cards are dealt singly and face down, except the last card, which is turned up. The suit of this card is the trump suit for the hand and the card is claimed by the dealer at their first turn. Players can agree to correct any misdeal unless anyone claims a redeal.

PLAYING
The player to the left of the dealer leads with one card. The other players follow suit in turn with one card. If a player cannot follow suit, they may play any other card. The trick is won by the highest trump card or the highest card of the leading suit.

The winner claims the trick by turning it face down near them and leading the next trick.

Play continues until 13 tricks have been made. The cards are then shuffled and dealt by the next person in clockwise direction from the first dealer.

Each person plays for themselves, but two players may form a temporary partnership in an attempt to reduce the lead of the third player.

SCORING

One point is scored for each trick taken. Points are deducted for tricks containing the following cards: The final score could be positive or negative.

J of hearts	4 points
J of diamonds	3 points
J of clubs	2 points
J of spades	1 point

WINNING THE GAME

The first person to gain 20 positive points is the winner.

Penalty cards

-4 points   -3 points   -2 points   -1 point

A simple form of whist for two to seven players, especially good for older children learning about tricks and trumps. A deck of standard cards is used with aces ranking high.

Rank

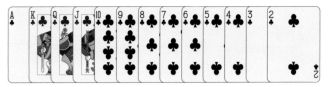

high   low

AIM
Everyone aims to win all the tricks of a hand and to avoid being eliminated from the game.

TRUMP SUIT
At each deal one suit becomes the trump suit; cards of that suit beat those of other suits.

TRICKS

A trick is a group of cards, one played by each person in turn. The suit of the first card played to a trick is called the leading suit. The trick is won by the highest card of the leading suit.

The highest cards are aces, then Ks, Qs, Js, 10s and so on down to 3s and 2s. If the leading suit is not the trump suit, a trump card takes the trick.

Some tricks made by four players

trump
suit

trick won by
Q clubs

trick won by
5 trumps

DEALING

Clockwise, one person deals each player seven cards, one at a time and face down. The rest of the cards are piled face down in the centre of the table and the top card turned over. The suit of this card is trumps for that deal.

At each new deal players' hands have one fewer card.

PLAYING
Players sort their cards into suits in rank order. The player on the left of the dealer plays one card face up to start the first trick. The other players in turn add a card, following suit. If they cannot, they may use a trump card or play any other card. The trick is won by the person who:

a plays the highest trump card; or
b plays the highest card of the leading suit if trumps are not used. The winning player starts the next trick.

Play continues until all seven tricks have been made.

Anyone who has not won a trick then drops out. The person winning the most tricks in the round begins the next round.

WINNING THE GAME

If a person wins all the tricks in any round, they are the winner of the game. If all seven rounds of the game are played, players have only one card in the last round. The person winning this trick wins the game.

Linger longer

A good game for learning about trump cards. At least three or more players are needed, but four or six is best. A standard deck of cards is used, ace ranking high.

Rank

high   low

AIM
Players try to be the last left holding cards.

TRUMP SUIT
At each deal one suit becomes the trump suit; its cards beat those of other suits.

TRICKS
A trick is a group of cards, one played by each person in turn. The suit of the first card played to a trick is the

leading suit. If no trumps are played, the trick is won by the highest card of the leading suit.

The highest cards are aces, then Ks, Qs, Js, 10s and so on down to 3s and 2s.

DEALING
One person deals cards, singly and face down, to each player clockwise. Each person is dealt the same number as there are players. For example, six players have six cards each.

The rest of the cards are piled face down on the table.

Some tricks made by four players

trumps   trick won by ace hearts   trick won by 7 trumps

The dealer shows their last card to everyone and its suit becomes the trump suit for the game.

PLAYING

The player on the dealer's left leads the trick by playing one card face up. Everyone else plays one card to complete the trick.

Cards should follow the suit of the first card; otherwise a trump card or any other card can be played.

The trick is won by the person who:

a plays the highest trump card; or
b plays the highest card of the leading suit if trumps are not used.

The winning player collects their trick near them, takes a card from the stock pile and uses any of their cards to start the next trick.

Players continue as long as they have cards in their hand. A player whose hand runs out drops out of the game.

The winner is the last person in the game.

My ship sails

Easy to learn, this game is exciting when played at high speed. It is for four to seven players using one standard deck of cards, ace ranking high.

AIM
Players try to collect seven cards from the same suit, such as seven hearts.

DEALING
The dealer is the person who cuts the highest card.

Seven cards are dealt to each player, one at a time and face down, clockwise. The rest of the deck is not needed.

PLAYING
Players sort their cards by suits. They decide which suit to collect, although this can change as cards are exchanged.

EXCHANGING
Each person puts an unwanted card face down on

the table and slides it to the player on the right, who picks it up.

Each then discards another card, slides it to the right and picks up their own new card from the left.

This continues until one player's hand is all one suit and they shout 'My ship sails'. The first to do so is the winner.

My ship sails

Newmarket

Michigan, Boodle and Stops are alternative names for this popular card game, which mostly revolves around chance.

CARDS
One standard 52-card deck as well as an ace, king, queen and jack (one of each suit) from another deck to be used as the 'boodle' cards. Ace is high.

AIM
The object is to collect as many counters as possible, by getting rid of all the cards in a hand.

PLAYERS
The game works with 3–8 players.

PREPARING
You will need a number of counters, tokens or matchsticks to use as a stake. Each player receives the same number of these at the start of the game. A stake is agreed and players each put this in the kitty, plus an additional stake on each boodle card.

A good rule is to raise a kitty stake of between one and four times the total boodle stake.

DEALING
The dealer, who is picked at random, places the four boodle cards face-up in the middle of the table. They then deal the entire 52-card deck between all players and a 'dummy' hand, starting with the player to their left.

PLAYING
Play begins as whoever holds the two of diamonds announces it and places it in front of them. If no one has it (i.e. it is in the dummy hand), call for three, and so on. Play proceeds in this manner, the next highest card of the same suit being placed by (and in front of) the player who holds it and so on. This will continue until a card in the dummy hand is called. On these occasions, the last player to place a card will then choose their lowest card of another suit. If this player does not have a card of another suit, the player to their left resumes play. Whenever a boodle card is played, its player claims that card's boodle stake.

WINNING THE GAME

This process continues until someone becomes the first to have played an entire hand, thereby winning the kitty stake for that round.

The winner of the game is the person with the most counters after an agreed number of rounds or when one player has run out of counters.

Similar to whist, oh hell is a game for three or more players, each playing alone. Oh hell is also known as blackout, and by some as oh well.

CARDS
A standard 52-card deck is used, with ace ranking high.

Rank

high   low

AIM
Every player makes a bid for tricks, which they try to fulfil exactly.

DEALING
The player making the highest cut becomes the first dealer. Subsequent deals pass clockwise; there are several deals in each game. In the first deal players are

dealt one card each. In the next deal, players are dealt two cards each; in the third, three cards; and so on.

When it is no longer possible to deal an extra card to each player, the game ends. For example, when there are four players there will be 13 deals; when there are five players, 10 deals.

TRUMPS

The top card from the stock is turned up at the end of each deal to designate trumps. When the last deal of the game allows for no stock, there are no trumps in that hand.

BIDDING

The dealer begins by bidding the number of tricks they expect to win or bidding 'nullo' if they do not expect to make any.

In the first hand, the bid is one or nullo. The number of possible bids increases as the number of dealt cards increases.

PLAYING

The player to the dealer's left leads with any card. In the first hand they have no choice but to play the single card they have been dealt. The others must follow suit if they can. If not, they may trump or discard.

The player winning the trick claims it face down and leads to the next trick.

SCORING

Players who have fulfilled their bids exactly gain one point per trick plus a bonus of 10 points.

For fulfilling a bid of nullo, the score may be five points, or one point per trick in the hand plus five points. Players should agree beforehand which scoring system is to be used.

Players who make fewer or more than the number of tricks bid do not score or lose penalty points.

OPTIONAL SCORING

A bonus of 25 points can be won by a player who fulfils a small slam bid by winning all but one of the hand's tricks, providing there are more than five cards in the hand.

A bonus of 50 points can be won by a player who makes a grand slam (all the tricks).

WINNING THE GAME

The player with the highest total score after all deals are played is the winner.

An easy game for three or more young children, also called 'pass the lady'.

AIM
There are no winners. Instead, players try to avoid being the loser by getting rid of all their cards.

CARDS
A standard deck of 52 cards is used with one of the Qs removed. This leaves a deck with a pair of Qs in one colour and a single Q – the old maid – in the other.

Old maid

one Q removed   old maid   pair of Qs

DEALING
All the cards are dealt, face down and one at a time.

Hands might be unequal.

PLAYING

Players sort their cards, keeping them hidden from other players. Anyone holding pairs of matching cards puts them out face up. Pairs are two cards with the same number or picture.

If someone holds three matching cards, they only put down one pair and keep the odd card. If they have four, they put down two pairs.

The player to the left of the dealer spreads their cards in their hand, keeping them hidden. They offer them to the player on their left who takes one card. If the card matches one already held, they put down the pair. If not, they put it in their hand, and they in turn spread their cards for the player on their left.

The game continues in the same way until all the cards have been put down in pairs except the old maid, which cannot be paired. The person holding the card is called 'old maid' by the others and loses the game.

Developed from bezique, pinochle is a game for two players. It is popular in North America and is also known as pinocle or penuchle.

CARDS
Two standard 52-card decks are stripped of all cards below 9, leaving a deck of 48 cards. The cards rank ace, 10, K, Q, J and 9 from high to low.

Rank

high   low

AIM
Each person tries to make scoring melds and take tricks that contain high-scoring cards.

DEALING
The player making the highest cut becomes the first

dealer. They shuffle the cards and ask the non-dealer to cut them before they deal 12 cards to the non-dealer and themselves, in packets of three or four.

The trump suit for the hand is assigned by turning up the next card and placing it face up on the table.

If it is a 9, it is called the dix and the dealer gains 10 points immediately.

A stock is made by turning the remaining cards face down, partly obscuring the trump card. The same trump remains throughout both stages of play.

PLAYING: STAGE ONE
The non-dealer plays a card to the first trick, followed by the dealer, who may play any card and does not have to follow suit.

The trick is won by the highest trump card or by the highest ranking card of the leading suit, if no trumps are played. If both cards in the trick are of the same suit and denomination, the one played first wins.

The winner of the trick places it face down in front of them. They may then claim a meld if they wish.

MELDING

During the first stage of play, the winner of each trick may claim a meld by placing the appropriate cards face up on the table and calling its name and score.

MELDS

There are three classes of meld, with name and points values as shown.

Class A

Ace, 10, K, Q and J of trumps, 'sequence' or 'flush'	150 points
K and Q of trumps, 'royal marriage'	40 points
K and Q of a plain suit, 'marriage'	20 points

Class B

Q of spades and J of diamonds, 'pinochle'	40 points

Class C

Sets of four cards must contain one from each suit.

Four aces	100 points
Four Ks	80 points
Four Qs	60 points
Four Js	40 points

Melds when diamonds are trumps

Class A

150 points

40 points

20 points

Class B

40 points

Trump

Class C

100 points

80 points

60 points

40 points

Only one meld can be scored in each turn, although each melded card can be used to form a meld of a different class, or one of a higher score in the same class, at another turn. Each new meld formed from a previous meld must also contain a new card from the hand.

A player may use any of their melded cards to make tricks, but cards used for tricks cannot be used again to make melds.

DRAWING FROM THE STOCK

Whether they have made a meld or not, the player completes their turn by taking the top card from the stock. The other player then takes the next card from the stock.

The first stage of play continues until all the stock (including the trump card) has been taken. An optional rule of play is that the last face-down card should be revealed by whoever takes it.

THE DIX

The 9 of trumps is called the dix. If it was not turned up by the dealer and instead appears during the first stage of play, the person holding it may declare it, lay it down on the table and claim 10 points. It is usual to allow a meld to be made in the same turn. After winning a trick, the player may exchange the dix for the trump card under the stock.

PLAYING: STAGE TWO

Known as the playout, this stage requires each player to take back into their hand all the cards that remain in their melds on the table.

The player who won the last trick of the first stage leads a card for the first of 12 tricks in this stage.

The other player must follow suit if they can. If not, they may play a trump or discard. If the leading card is a trump, a higher trump must be played, if possible. Usually, the player following the lead tries to take the trick if they can.

No melds are made and the winner of one trick leads to the next.

SCORING TRICKS

At the end of each hand, tricks are scored according to the cards taken, as follows:

a	Ace	11 points each
b	10	10 points each
c	K	4 points each
d	Q	3 points each
e	J	2 points each

Points for tricks are rounded up to the nearest multiple of 10 if the units are 7, 8, 9 and rounded down if the units are below 7.

The player winning the final trick of the second stage of play gains an extra 10 points.

Scoring tricks

11 points   10 points   4 points   3 points   2 points

WINNING THE GAME

The player who first reaches a score of 1000 points wins the game. If both players pass the 1000-point total in the same hand, they play on until one reaches a score of 1250. If a draw happens again, play continues until 1500 points have been won, and so on, until there is one clear winner.

Piquet

This game offers two players the opportunity to use great skill. Known by various names since the 1450s, the game was given its French name and terminology by Charles I of England to honour Henrietta Maria, his French wife.

Modern piquet has some optional rules, sometimes called American style or English style. The options are described here when they occur. Most players generally choose one style and keep to it.

CARDS
The piquet deck of 32 cards is used, which ranks normally with ace high. It is made by stripping the cards below 7 from a standard 52-card deck. Regular piquet players have two decks, one in use and the other ready shuffled for the next deal.

Rank

high   low

AIM

A player tries to score more points than their opponent by taking tricks and by collecting scoring combinations of cards.

Card values

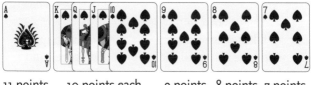

11 points   10 points each   9 points   8 points   7 points

DEALING

The player cutting the higher card becomes first dealer and chooses their seat. The dealer shuffles the cards which are then cut by the non-dealer.

Beginning with the non-dealer, each player is dealt 12 cards in packets of two. A stock is formed from the remaining eight cards by turning the cards face down and dividing them so that the upper five lie at an angle to the lower three.

THE PARTIE

A game is known as a partie and normally consists of six deals. Each deal has four parts:

a making discards;
b deciding which scoring combinations to declare;
c announcing declarations; and
d playing for tricks.

Scoring takes place as the partie unfolds, so paper and pencil are essential for keeping the scores and cumulative totals.

SCORING BEFORE THE DISCARD

After the deal, and before a player discards, they may claim 10 points if they have been dealt carte blanche (a hand with no court cards). English rules state a carte blanche score must be claimed before both players discard.

MAKING DISCARDS

The dealer discards first. American rules state that they need not discard, but English rules say they must discard at least one card. Either way, a player may only discard up to five cards. If the dealer decides to discard, they place the cards they want to discard face down near them.

Drawing from the top of the stock, in order, they take the same number of cards into their hand.

If the dealer chooses not to discard, or discards fewer than five cards, they have the right to look at all five top cards of the stock, replacing them in the same order. They do not show the cards to their opponent.

The non-dealer must then discard one card and may discard more, up to the number remaining in the whole stock. They place the cards face down beside them and take replacements into their hand from the top of the stock in order.

They can then inspect the cards (if any) that remain in the stock, but if they do, the dealer may also inspect them. (Some players only allow the dealer to inspect them later, after they have played their first trick.)

During play, both players may inspect their own discards at any time.

COMBINATIONS TO DECLARE

Players can make three kinds of combinations, using the cards in their hands. Any card may be included in more than one combination. The aim is to make high-scoring combinations which rank higher than the opponent's combinations.

A player may choose to 'sink' one or more of their combinations by not declaring it. No score can be claimed for any combination that has been sunk.

There are three types of combination, called 'point', 'sequence' and 'meld'.

A point is a collection of cards all of the same suit. The player with the biggest collection scores one point for each card in that suit.

If both players have a collection of the same number, the cards in each collection are counted at face value and the highest score wins the point value. If there is still a draw, neither player scores. A player can only score for one point, even if they hold two collections greater than their opponent's.

Ranking when point scores are the same

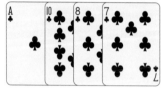 

point score is 4
face value is 36
this point ranks higher

point score is 4
face value is 35
this point ranks lower

A sequence is a run of three or more cards in one suit in rank order. The player with the longest sequence scores for all the sequences they hold, as follows:

a	Three cards, a tierce	3 points
b	Four cards, a quart	4 points
c	Five cards, a quint	15 points
d	Six cards, a sextet or sixième	16 points
e	Seven cards, a septet or septième	17 points
f	Eight cards, an octet or huitième	18 points

The loser makes no score for any of their sequences.

If there is a draw, the sequence with the highest ranking top card wins. If there is still a draw, neither player scores.

Sample sequences in rank order

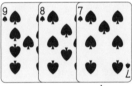

lowest rank: 3 points

highest rank: 15 points

A meld is three or four cards of the same kind in different suits. Only aces, Ks, Qs, Js and 10s may be used in melds. Some players only allow 10s in melds of four cards.

The player making the longest meld scores for all the melds they hold as follows:

<blockquote>

a three cards, a trio   3 points

b four cards, a quatorze or 'fourteen' 14 points

</blockquote>

If both players have melds of the same length, the one with the highest ranking cards wins.

Sample melds

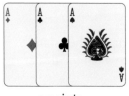

3 points

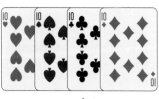

14 points

ANNOUNCING DECLARATIONS

The announcements are made briefly and formally to avoid revealing too much information. Declarations are made in the order of points, sequences and then melds. (Some players prefer the French names for sequences and melds.) The non-dealer begins each dialogue.

DIALOGUE DECLARING A POINT

Non-dealer: 'A point of...,' saying how many cards are in their longest suit. Dealer replies with either:

a 'Good' if they concede the point;
b 'Not good...,' stating how many cards in their point if it is longer; or
c 'How many?' if their suit is the same length. Non-dealer continues with either:
a 'A point of... I score...,' restating their point and its score;
b 'Good' conceding the point; or
c if the dealer had asked 'How many?' they state the face value of their point, to which the dealer replies:
a 'Good' conceding the point;
b 'Not good...,' stating the face value of their point if greater and claiming the point score; or
c 'Equal' if the face value is the same. In this case, neither player scores.

The player who wins the point always ends by saying: 'A point of... I score...,' giving the point value and its score.

DECLARING A SEQUENCE

Non-dealer: 'A sequence of…,' stating the number of cards in their longest one.

The dealer replies with either 'Good,' 'Not good' or 'How high?' and the dialogue continues as for points. The reply to 'How high?' is to name the top card of the sequence.

DECLARING A MELD

The non-dealer begins by declaring 'a three (or a fourteen) of…,' stating the denomination of their meld. The reply can only be 'Good' or 'Not good' as players cannot have equal melds.

A SAMPLE DECLARATION

The declarations of points, sequences and melds follow each other.

Non-dealer: 'A point of four.'

Dealer: 'Good.'

Non-dealer: 'A point of four. I score four. A quint (sequence of five).'

Dealer: 'How high?'

Non-dealer: 'Jack.'

Dealer: 'Not good. Queen. Also a tierce (a sequence of three). I score eight.'

Non-dealer: 'A trio of queens (three queens).'

Dealer: 'Not good. A quatorze (fourteen in kings). I score fourteen. I start with 22.'

Non-dealer: 'I start with five.' They scored four for their point plus one for leading the first trick (see Scoring tricks).

A SAMPLE OF ENGLISH-STYLE DECLARATION
The dealer only declares their combinations after the non-dealer has led the first trick.

Non-dealer: 'A point of four.'

Dealer: 'Good.'

Non-dealer: 'A point of four. I score four. A sequence of five.'

Dealer: 'How high?'

Non-dealer: 'Jack.'

Dealer: 'Not good.'

Non-dealer: 'A trio of queens.'

Dealer: 'Not good.'

The non-dealer then plays the leading card to the first trick, saying: 'I start with five.'

The dealer then makes their declarations: 'A quart to queen, also a tierce. Eight. A quatorze of kings. Fourteen. I start with 22.'

SHOWING COMBINATIONS
It is sometimes ruled that all the winning combinations must be shown before they are scored.

However, it is standard practice for a player to request their opponent to show their combination, which is immediately replaced in the hand. If an opponent does not request a show, none is given.

PLAYING

The first trick is led by the non-dealer. Players must follow suit if possible. If not, any card may be discarded. The player winning the trick leads to the next one.

SCORING TRICKS

a	For leading to a trick	1 point
b	For taking a trick led by the opponent	1 point
c	For taking the last trick	1 point
d	For taking seven or more tricks	10 points

Every time a player scores, they record it and announce their running total. There are some optional variations to scoring for tricks:

1 a player only scores for leading to a trick if the leading card is 10 or higher;
2) a player only scores for winning a trick if the winning card is 10 or higher.

SCORING ADDITIONAL POINTS

a	Carte blanche (a hand with no court cards at the deal)	10 points
b	Pique (a score of 30 points by the non-dealer before the dealer scores anything)	30 points
c	Repique (a score of 30 points by either player before the lead to the first trick)	60 points
d	Capot (taking all 12 tricks during play)	40 points

The player cannot also claim the 10 points for taking seven or more tricks (see Scoring tricks).

SCORING THE PARTIE (GAME)

1 The scores for each deal are added together to give players their individual total. If a partie consists of six games, six totals will be added. Some people prefer a partie of four games. In this case the scores for the first and the last deals are doubled before the four totals are added.

2 If both players have reached or exceeded the rubicon (100 points), the winner is the player with the higher total. The winner's score then becomes the difference between the two players' totals, plus a bonus of 100 points for winning the partie.

3 If one or both players have totals of fewer than 100 points, the player with the lower total is 'rubiconed'. The other player is the winner and their score then becomes the sum of the two players' totals, plus a bonus of 100 points for winning the partie.

Sample scores	Totals	Final score	
Dealer	120	120-108+100 = 112	Winner
Non-dealer	108	Nil	
Dealer	95	Nil	
Non-dealer	125	125+95+100 = 325	Winner
Dealer	82	Nil	
Non-dealer	85	85+82+100 = 267	Winner

Play or pay

A game using rank and sequence for three or more players. It is also called round the corner.

AIM
Players try to win counters by getting rid of their cards in each round.

DEALING
Each deal is one round of the game. Players should agree how many rounds will make the game.

One player deals all the cards clockwise from a standard deck, one at a time and face down. Players might not have equal numbers.

Each player also starts with 20 counters.

PLAYING
The player on the dealer's left plays one card face up. The next player, on their left, looks to see if they can follow that card with one in the same suit in sequence: ace, 2, 3, 4, 5, 6, 7, 8, 9, 10, J, Q, K.

If the card played is the K, the sequence goes 'round the corner' to the ace of that suit.

If a player holds the next card in sequence, they play it face up on top of the last card. If they do not, they must pay one counter into the middle of the table.

The person playing the last card of a suit then plays any card from their hand to start the next one.

WINNING THE GAME
The winner of the round is the first person to play all their cards. They take all the counters from the centre. Losers each pay them one counter for every card they still hold.

The winner of the game is the person with the most counters after the agreed number of rounds.

Cards in sequence

Pontoon

Pontoon is the British domestic version of the American blackjack or the French vingt-et-un.

CARDS
One standard 52-card deck.

AIM
The object of the game is to get closer than the banker to 21, as often as possible.

PLAYERS
Any number of players is suitable for pontoon.

PREPARING
You will need a number of counters, tokens or matchsticks to use as a stake. Each player receives the same number of these at the start of the game. Minimum and maximum stakes for each hand must be decided at the start of play.

Deal the cards face-up and the first person to be dealt a jack becomes the banker. This player remains the banker until another player gets a pontoon and takes over.

SCORING
All non-bankers are hoping for a hand as close to 21 as possible without going over that number. In this game, an ace can count as either one or 11 points (whichever suits the player and hand concerned), the court cards are worth 10, and the rest have face value. The best possible hand is a two-card 21 – also known as pontoon – of an ace plus a 10 or royal card. The next best thing is a five-card trick, which means a hand of five cards with any total value under or equal to 21.

DEALING
To begin, all players including the banker are dealt one card, face-down, by the banker. Players except the banker then look at their cards and place a stake within the minimum and maximum limits. The banker then deals them all a second card and, starting with the player on the banker's left, each player must make a choice as to their next move.

PLAYING

The playing options are:

- Pontoon: Turn the ace face-up, place it on top of the other card and pass the turn.
- Stick: No more cards will be dealt to this hand, which must total at least 15.
- Twist: The banker will turn the next card from the pile face up to be added to the hand in question. If the total remains under 21, a fourth and then fifth card can be added in the same way if desired.
- Buy a card: A further stake must be paid to receive another card from the banker. This can be done up to three times. Buying always happens before twisting, never after.
- Split: If a player holds two cards of the same value, turn both cards face-up and place a stake on each. The banker then deals one more face-down card on each and both hands can be played as normal.

If at any point the total value of a hands exceeds 21, the player concerned must turn the cards face-up and announce that they have gone bust. These cards will be added to the bottom of the pack by the banker and the player's stake will be collected.

At the end of this phase, all players will have either announced a pontoon, gone bust, or stuck with five cards totaling from 15 to 21.

The banker now turns over their own cards and either sticks or twists to their satisfaction. All other players turn over their cards and the banker pays out counters to match the stakes of players who have won, and collects the stakes of those who have lost. If the banker deals a card to their own hand that takes it over 21, they have gone bust. In this case the banker must pay an amount equal to their stake to all players still in the game, or a double stake for pontoons and/ or five card tricks.

WINNING THE GAME

The best hand wins. This means the hand closest to 21 or, if 21 is reached by more than one player, the winner is determined according to the following rankings:

1. Banker's pontoon
2. Pontoon
3. Five card trick

A game for three or more players in which cards are played in order to gain counters. Once very popular in Scotland, Pope Joan is a combination of two earlier games called commit and matrimony.

CARDS
The 8 of diamonds is removed from a standard deck, leaving 51 cards. Aces rank low and the 9 of diamonds is known as Pope Joan.

Rank

Pope Joan

high   low

PREPARING

Each player should begin with an equal number of counters with which to bet. A betting layout or board with eight sections will be needed. Some traditional boards for Pope Joan are revolving circular trays divided into eight segments. For a modern board, a square layout with eight sections can be drawn on paper or card as shown. The sections should be labelled king, queen, jack, ace, matrimony, game, intrigue and Pope Joan. They should be large enough to hold about 20 counters each.

Square layout

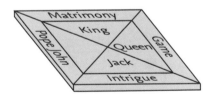

AIM

Certain cards are played in order to win counters. The player first using up all their cards also wins counters.

BETTING

A dealer is chosen by agreement. All players then place counters on the betting layout in one of two ways, again by agreement:

a everyone places the same number of counters on each section; or

b everyone places four players on Pope Joan, two on intrigue, two on matrimony and one on each of the other five sections.

Betting

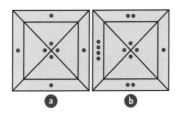

DEALING

The cards are dealt clockwise, one at a time and face down, beginning with the player to the dealer's left. An extra hand is dealt immediately before the dealer's own hand. All but one card is dealt out. This last card is placed exposed on top of the widow.

THE EXPOSED CARD

The standard rule is that if this exposed card is Pope Joan (9 of diamonds), all the counters in the game and pope sections of the board go to the dealer. Alternatively, some players agree the dealer should win all counters on the layout. Either way, that round ends and the deal passes to the player on the dealer's left.

If the exposed card is any card other than Pope Joan, its suit is the trump suit for that round.

If the exposed card is an ace or a court card, all counters on the corresponding section of the board go to the dealer, and the round continues.

PLAYING

The extra hand may not be inspected. The player to the dealer's left plays any card from their hand face up in the centre of the table, announcing its name – e.g. '3 of clubs'. The player holding the 4 of clubs plays and announces it. Then the players with the 5, the 6 and so on play those cards. A player holding two or more cards in sequence plays them all, announcing each one. The sequence continues until:

a the K has been reached and the sequence is complete;

b the next card would need to be the 8 of diamonds; or

c the next card has already been played or is hidden in the extra hand.

The sequence is then turned face down and may not be inspected. The person playing the last card begins another sequence with any card from their hand.

CLAIMING COUNTERS

Certain cards win counters when played in correct sequence.

The ace, J, Q or K of trumps win all the counters on the section of the same name. The J and Q of trumps, played in sequence, win the counters on the intrigue, jack and queen sections.

The Q and K of trumps, played together, win the counters on matrimony, queen and king.

If Pope Joan is played, the player claims the counters on that section, whether it is the trump suit or not.

None of these cards can score if they remain in the hand.

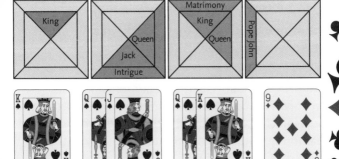

ENDING A ROUND
When someone has played all their cards, the round ends and they take the counters from the game section. All other players pay them one counter for each card they are still holding. The only exemption is a player left holding Pope Joan, who does not pay for any cards in their hand. At the end of each round,

unclaimed counters remain in place. At the beginning of each round, counters are added before the deal.

WINNING THE GAME
The game usually continues to an agreed time limit. Then a final deal is made, excluding the extra hand and including the last card, to determine who shall claim any remaining counters.

The players receiving the ace, J, Q and K of diamonds, and the Pope Joan, claim the counters on those sections. Any counters in matrimony are shared between the players holding the K and Q of diamonds; counters in intrigue go equally to the holders of the J and Q.

Racing demon

A noisy game – also known as fighting patience – for any number that is played at great speed and requires a lot of space.

AIM
Players try to use all 13 cards in their piles and play as many cards as they can into the middle.

CARDS
Each player needs a complete deck of 52 cards. Old cards with different backs are the best.

DEALING
Players shuffle their own decks and deal themselves 13 cards face down. The pile is turned up and four more cards are dealt face up side by side with it. Players keep their remaining cards face down in one hand.

PLAYING
One person is the starter who shouts 'go' to start the game once everyone has dealt. Players put cards into the centre or on their own row of four cards as fast as they can.

PLAYING INTO THE CENTRE

If a player has an ace, this should be put face up in the centre. The 2 of the same suit, followed by the 3, 4, 5, 6, 7, 8, 9, 10, J, Q, K in that order, can then be played by the person holding them.

PLAYING ONTO THE FOUR FACE-UP CARDS

Each player can play onto their own row of four cards but must play in descending order, alternating black and red cards. For example, red K, black Q, or black 9, red 8, black 7 and so on.

WHICH CARDS CAN BE PLAYED

a The top card from the 13 pile.

b A card or a sequence of cards from one of any other face-up piles. Gaps made by doing this are filled with the top card from the pile of 13.

c If neither of the above is possible, the player turns three cards over from the spare pile in their hand to make a new face-up pile. This is continued until the player gets a card they can play. When the spare pile runs out, the face-up pile is turned over to use as a spare pile.

ENDING THE GAME

A player shouts 'out' as soon as they have used up all the cards from their original pile of 13.

SCORING

The cards from the centre are sorted into their different decks. Each player counts how many cards are left in their original face-up piles. Their final score is this number subtracted from the number from their deck in the centre. The player with the highest score is the winner.

Rolling stone

A popular game with unexpected moments for four, five or six players.

AIM
Players try to get rid of their cards.

CARDS
One standard deck is used with the 2s removed for six players; 2s, 3s and 4s removed for five; and 2s, 3s, 4s, 5s, and 6s, removed for four. Aces rank high.

Rank

high   low

DEALING
Players cut; highest cut deals all the cards clockwise, one at a time, so that each player has eight cards.

PLAYING

Players sort their cards by suit. The player to the left of the dealer plays one card face up. The next player on their left must play a card of the same suit (follow suit).

Each player in turn plays one card following suit and the group of cards, or trick, is piled face down. The person who played the highest card starts the next round.

If a player cannot follow suit, they pick up all the cards played for that trick, adding them to their hand. They start the next trick from the cards they already held.

The player to run out of cards first is the winner.

Rummy

Internationally one of the most popular card games, rummy evolved from rum poker, which was played in 19th-century saloons in the USA.

PLAYERS
Any number from two to six, everyone playing for themselves.

CARDS
The standard deck of 52 cards is used and ace ranks low. J, Q and K of each suit are worth 10 points each; all other cards are face value, with ace worth one point. Melds are made by:

a grouping three or four cards of the same rank; or
b making a sequence of three or more cards of the same suit.

Melds

a group

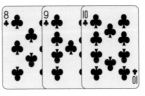

b sequence

AIM

Individuals try to be first to go out by melding all their cards.

PREPARING

The first dealer is chosen by low cut. They then shuffle the cards and invite the player on their right to cut the pack. A winning score is agreed (see Scoring) and scores are kept on paper.

DEALING

Cards are dealt singly in clockwise rotation, the number depending on how many players there are:

a two players are each dealt 10 cards;
b three to four players are each dealt 7 cards;
c five to six players are each dealt 6 cards. A stock is made by turning the pile of undealt cards face down. A discard pile is begun by turning up the top card from the stock and placing this upcard on the table, next to the stock.

PLAYING

The player to the left of the dealer begins by choosing to take either the upcard or the top card from the stock. They may then lay face up on the table any meld they hold. Finally, a card must be discarded. This can be any card except the one taken from the discard pile. Play proceeds clockwise. After laying down melds, players may additionally lay off extra cards on melds already formed by other players.

The round ends when a player goes out – i.e. uses up all their cards, with or without a final discard. A player goes rummy when they go out all in one hand without any previous melding or laying off of cards.

If no player has gone out before the stock is used up, a new stock is made by turning the discard pile face down, without shuffling.

After a player has gone out, there is a new deal for the next round. The deal passes clockwise from the first dealer.

SCORING
When a player goes out, their score is the combined numerical value of all their opponents' cards in hand. When a player goes rummy, the score is doubled.

WINNING THE GAME
The first player to reach the agreed score wins the match.

Scotch whist

Not at all like whist, this game is often called catch the ten.

PLAYERS
Any number from two to six people each play for themselves. If there are four players, they may prefer to play in partnerships.

CARDS
A deck of 36 cards is made by stripping all the 2s, 3s, 4s and 5s from a standard 52-card deck. Ace ranks high in both plain and trump suits, but the J ranks highest when a suit is trumps. A trick consists of one card from each person played in turn.

Rank when spades are trumps

high   low

Rank when spades is a plain suit

high   low

AIM
Each player tries to win as many tricks as they can, especially those containing high-scoring trump cards.

DEALING

The player making the highest cut becomes the first dealer and decides the seating positions. They shuffle the cards, inviting the player on their right to cut the cards.

Beginning with the player on their left and proceeding clockwise, they deal cards singly, face down. If there are two or three players, each is dealt 10 cards.

If there are four or more players, the whole deck is dealt. When there are four players they receive nine cards each, and the last card dealt to the dealer is turned up to determine the trump suit for that hand.

Five players will be dealt seven cards each, and the 36th card will be turned up to determine trumps before being dealt to the next player in turn, who will then have a hand of eight cards. Six players will receive six cards each and the dealer's last card will determine trumps.

PLAYING

The player to the left of the dealer begins by playing any card from their hand. Players follow suit in turn. If they cannot follow suit, they may trump or discard.

The trick is won by:
a the highest trump card; or
b the highest card of the leading suit.

The player winning a trick leads to the next one. Play continues in this way until all cards have been played. If there are five players, the final trick will consist of six cards.

SCORING

At the end of a hand, certain trump cards earn points. Players holding these cards can score for them as follows:

J of trumps	11 points
10 of trumps	10 points
Ace of trumps	4 points
K of trumps	3 points
Q of trumps	2 points

Players also score one card point for every card taken in tricks in excess of the number they were dealt. For example:

dealt 10, taken 15 in tricks: 5 points

dealt 6, taken 18 in tricks: 12 points

If a player fails to follow the rules of play, they are not allowed to score in that deal and have 10 points deducted from their score.

WINNING THE GAME
The first person who reaches a score of 41 points wins the game. If two players reach a total of 41 in the same hand, the winner is decided by scoring the points in this order: 10 of trumps, card points, ace, K, Q and J of trumps.

Sequence

Easy to learn, this game uses some skill. Best with four or five players, but as few as two can play.

AIM
Players try to get rid of their cards, and collect counters, by playing on sequences.

CARDS
A standard deck of cards is used. Cards are ranked in numerical order: 2, 3, 4, 5, 6, 7, 8, 9, 10, J, Q, K, ace.

Cards all of the same suit make up a sequence.

A sequence

high   low

DEALING

One player deals the whole deck one at a time, face down and clockwise. Some players may hold unequal numbers of cards. Each player also begins with 10 counters, and the number of rounds is agreed.

PLAYING

The player to the dealer's left plays their lowest card face up on the table. The player who holds the next card (or cards) in sequence plays it.

Play continues until all the cards of that sequence have been played, from the 2 up to the ace. The next sequence is begun by whoever played the last card. The winner is the player who is first to get rid of all their cards.

SCORING

At the end of a round, the losers pay the winner one counter for every card they hold. The winner of the game is the one with the most counters after all the rounds.

Seven up

A 17th-century English game for two or three players, seven up is also known as high-low-jack, all fours and old sledge.

CARDS
A standard deck of 52 cards is used, the ace ranking high.

Rank

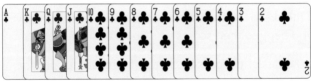

high   low

AIM
Players try to win the game by scoring seven points.

DEALING
The first dealer is the player making the highest cut, and they deal six cards, face down, to each player in two packets of three.

The next card is turned face up to indicate the trump suit. If it is any of the Js, the dealer wins one point. Subsequent deals pass clockwise around the table

THE TRUMP SUIT

The player to the dealer's left calls 'stand' if they are satisfied with the trump suit. Play then begins. If not, they say 'I beg' and the dealer has to choose to keep or to change trumps.

If they keep the trumps, they reply 'take one'. The player who begged then scores one point and play begins.

If the dealer chooses to change trumps, they put the face-up card to one side and deal a packet of three more cards to each player, turning the next card up to indicate the new trump suit.

If it is the same suit as the first trump, then the dealer repeats the procedure of dealing another three cards to each player and turning up the next card, until a new suit is indicated as trumps. If the deck runs out before a new trump is turned up, the cards are thrown in, shuffled and redealt. If the extra deal produces a new trump suit, play begins. If this card is a J, the dealer wins a point, providing it is not of the same suit as the first trump.

DISCARDING
After the trump has been set, players must discard all but six cards from their hands.

PLAYING
Play is the same as whist. The player to the left of the dealer plays one card to lead to the first trick. Players must each follow suit if possible. If not, they may use a trump or discard.

The winner of one trick leads to the next one. Play continues until all six tricks are made. Each player claims their own tricks, keeping the cards near them, face down.

SCORING
Tricks are turned face up for scoring at the end of each round. One point can be won for each of the following:

a) a 'high' (to the player dealt the highest trump);
b) a 'low' (to the player dealt the lowest trump);
c) a 'jack' (to the player who takes a trick containing the J of trumps); and
d) 'game' (to the player with the highest value of cards won in tricks). Cards each carry a points value as follows:

Ace	4 points
K	3 points
Q	2 points
J	1 point
10	10 points

WINNING THE GAME

The game is won by the first player to make seven points. If there is a draw of seven points each in the same hand, the points are counted in order, as follows, to decide who is the winner: high, low, jack, game.

Snap

A very popular, noisy game of great fun for two or more players.

AIM
Everyone tries to take all the cards.

CARDS
An old, standard deck is fun to use, although special snap cards are available. Two decks are better for more than three players. If some are missing, it does not matter.

DEALING
All the cards are dealt out by one player, singly and face down in a clockwise direction. Players do not look at their cards. It does not matter if some players have more than others. Everyone piles their cards in front of them, face down.

PLAYING
The player on the left of the dealer turns their top card over and puts it face down next to their own pile.

The next player on their left does the same, making another upturned pile of their own. All the other players do the same in turn.

When a player runs out of face-down cards they turn their face-up pile down and continue.

SNAP
When one player sees that the cards on top of two piles match, such as two 8s or two Ks, they shout 'snap!'

The first to do so collects both the piles which have the matched cards and adds them to the bottom of their own face-down pile.

Play continues with the person to the left of the last person to turn over a card.

THE SNAP POOL
When two players shout snap at the same time, the two piles of cards are placed together in the centre and are called the snap pool.

Play continues as before. When someone turns up a card that matches the card on top of the pool, they shout 'snap pool!' and takes the whole pool.

PENALTY

Everyone should agree which penalty is to be paid when a player incorrectly calls snap:

a the player pays each person one card from their face-down pile; or
b the player's face-down pile is turned over, placed in the centre and becomes a snap pool.

The winner is the one player left with cards.

A fast, hilarious game for three or more players using a standard deck of cards.

AIM
Everyone tries to get rid of their cards.

DEALING
Players cut; highest cut is the dealer. Ace is high in this game.

All the cards are dealt one at a time, face down and clockwise. Some players may have more than others.

PLAYING
Players sort their cards, putting together cards that match each other in order, such as two 4s, a 5, four 6s, one 7, two 10s, three Js and so on.

The player to the left of the dealer plays one card face up in the centre.

If the next player to the left has a card that matches, they put it down and shout 'snip!' If they have another matching card they must wait for their next turn to play it. If they cannot play a card they say 'pass'.

Play continues in turn, clockwise, until a player puts the third matching card in the centre. They shout 'snap!' The player to put down the fourth matching card shouts 'snorem!' They then start the next round.

WINNING THE GAME
The first player to get rid of all their cards is the winner.

Sample play

Snip!   Snap!   Snorem!

Solitaire (Patience)

Most likely originating in Germany or Scandinavia but made popular in 19th-century France, this game involves manipulating a layout of cards so that they can be sorted and removed (or sent back to the 'foundation'). Variants include patience, solitaire, klondike and the computerised FreeCell.

CARDS
One standard 52-card deck.

AIM
The object of the game is to clear the tableau and build up four foundation piles in suit, running from ace to king.

PLAYERS
Patience is generally a single-player game, though it can be played competitively by, for example, aiming to be the first to complete the foundations (usually against one other player, each having their own deck and tableau).

DEALING
Deal a tableau of seven columns, each increasing in length by one card from the first, single-card column on

the left to the seventh, seven-card column on the right. This should be dealt in rows from left to right, with the first card in each row (and therefore last in each column) being placed face-up. The first card dealt, face-up, constitutes the first column and is followed in a row by six cards face-down. The following row begins with a face-up card on the second column and five face-down cards on the subsequent columns, and so on until the seventh row has seven cards.

PLAYING

A card can only be moved onto another that is one rank higher and of an alternate colour. For example, a six of hearts could be placed either on a seven of clubs or a seven of spades. This move can only be made when the card is either at the bottom of a column, or is followed in its column by cards in the same decreasing, alternate order (e.g. a black and red alternating run from five down to two). When a face-down card is freed, it may be turned over and when a column is cleared, the space can be used for any other single card or sequence.

When all available moves have been made within the dealt tableau, draw three cards from the remaining deck and place them face-up in a new pile. Attempt to play the first of these and, only if successful, move onto the following face-up card. When a card cannot be used in the tableau, take another three cards from the remaining deck. Repeat this process until you have either exhausted all options or successfully re-ordered all cards within the tableau.

When an ace is freed up, move it to become the start of a face-up foundation above the tableau. Foundations are built according to suit and run from ace to king.

WINNING THE GAME
When all four foundations are complete, the game is won. If at any point, however, you find yourself unable to play any more legal moves, the game is up.

Spit

A fast-moving game for two people who enjoy being alert. A standard deck of cards is used.

AIM
Both players try to get rid of all their cards.

DEALING
All the cards are dealt equally, one at a time, to each player. Players put down cards in front of them as follows:

a beginning from the left, three cards are placed face down in a row, then a fourth card is placed face up;

b beginning from the left again, another face-down card is placed on the first and second cards and a face-up card on the third;

c a face-down card is then placed on the first pile and a face-up card on the second;

d finally a face-up card is placed on the first pile.

Players put their remaining cards in a pile, face down to the left of their rows.

PLAYING

When both are ready, one player shouts 'spit!' Both players take the top card from their spare pile and put them face up in the centre, next to each other.

PLAYING TO THE CENTRE

With as much speed as possible, both players play as many cards from their face-up rows as they can onto the centre cards.

The card must be in sequence, up or down. For example, if the centre card is 10, then a J or 9 can be put on it (a 2 or a K can be played onto an ace). If a face-down card is revealed, it is turned up.

SPIT

Play continues in this way until neither can lay down any more cards on the centre. When this happens, one of them shouts 'spit!' Both players put a card from the top of their spare pile face up onto the central pile they started. Play then continues. If neither can continue, one shouts 'spit' again and they each put another card on the centre from their spare piles. If a player's spare pile runs out and they want to call spit, they turn their central pile over, shout 'spit' and continue to play using it as a spare pile.

ENDING A ROUND

A player should shout 'out' as soon as they have played all the cards from their face-up row. They win the round.

They pick up their spare pile, and the other player picks up both central piles and the cards left in their row, adding the cards under their spare pile.

STARTING ANOTHER ROUND
Both players lay down a row of cards as in the first round. Play continues in the same way as before with one exception. After the first round, if a player's spare pile runs out they play without it and both people play onto the same pile in the centre.

WINNING THE GAME
The first player to get rid of all their cards wins the game.

Stealing bundles

Also called stealing the old man's bundle, this game is for two to four players using one standard deck of cards. Young children able to match cards of the same rank will enjoy it.

AIM
Players try to collect the most cards.

DEALING
One player deals each player four cards, singly and face down in a clockwise direction. The next four cards are then put face up in a row in the centre. The rest of the deck is put face down to one side.

PLAYING
The player to the left of the dealer looks to see if they have a card that matches in rank one in the centre. If they have, they capture the centre card and put it face up with their own near them. This is their 'bundle'.

If a player's card is the same rank as two or three centre cards, they can capture them all at the same time. If a player's card is the same rank as the top card in somebody's bundle, they can capture the whole bundle. If none of a player's cards matches any centre card they must 'trail', or put one of their own cards face up in the centre.

Everyone plays a card in turn. Whenever cards are captured, they are put on the bundle with the matching card face up.

Cards of the same rank

EXTRA DEALS
When everyone has played all of their four cards, four more cards are dealt to each player, and none to the centre, and the game continues.

WINNING THE GAME
When all the cards have been dealt and played, the player with the most cards in their bundle wins.

War

An easy introduction to card playing, war is for two players using a standard deck of cards. It can be varied for three players.

AIM
Everyone tries to get all the cards.

DEALING
One person deals the whole deck one at a time face down. Both players put their cards face down in a pile without looking at them.

PLAYING
Each player turns over the top card of their pile and puts it in the centre face up next to the other player's card. The player whose card is the higher ranking, regardless of suit, collects both cards and adds them to the bottom of their pile.

Players continue to turn over cards together and collect them.

Rank of cards in mixed suits

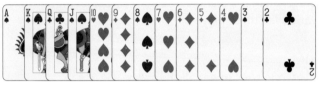

high   low

WAR

War occurs when two cards of the same rank are turned over.

Both players then put another card on top of their first card, but face down, and another face up. The higher ranking of the last two cards wins all six cards.

If these are the same rank, the war continues, and the player turning up the higher ranking card will claim 10 or more cards from the centre.

Playing war

player A

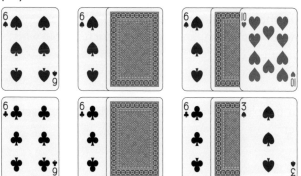

player B
player A wins all six cards

WINNING THE GAME
The game is won by:

a the player who wins all the cards; or
b the player with the most cards at the end of an
   agreed time limit.

Whist became popular when Edmond Hoyle described it in the first published rule book of card games in 1746. It was a refinement of the older game of triumph, sometimes called whisk. Whist has since spawned many challenging games such as solo whist and contract bridge.

PLAYERS
Four people play in pairs. Partners sit opposite each other.

CARDS
The standard deck of 52 is used. Ace ranks high. A set of four cards, one played in turn from each player, is a trick.

AIM
Partners cooperate to win tricks.

PREPARING
The first dealer is chosen by high cut for which ace ranks low. Any player can shuffle the cards before the

dealer makes the final shuffle and invites the player on their right to cut the pack.

DEALING

The whole pack is dealt in clockwise direction. Cards are dealt singly, face down, except the last one which is turned up to assign trumps for that hand. The dealer claims this card when they make their first play.

There is a misdeal if any player receives fewer or more than 13 cards or if any but the last card is revealed.

Players can agree to proceed after mistakes are corrected, or a redeal can be claimed before the first trick is played.

The redeal passes to the next player clockwise.

PLAYING

The first player to the left of the dealer leads the play by laying a card face up in the middle of the table.

Each person in turn plays one card of the leading suit face up. Anyone who cannot follow suit may use a trump or any other card.

The trick is won by the person playing:

a the highest trump card; or
b the highest ranking card of the leading suit.

Sample tricks

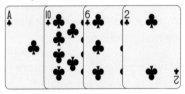

clubs are led; the Ace of clubs wins the trick

clubs are led; the 8 of clubs wins the trick

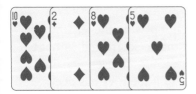

hearts are led; diamonds are trumps; the 2 of diamonds wins the trick

The winner claims the trick by turning it face down in front of them, and leads play for the next trick. The game continues until the hand of 13 tricks has been completed.

If all 13 tricks are won by one partnership, it is called a slam.

Subsequent deals for each new hand pass clockwise to the next player, who shuffles as before. A new trump suit is declared at each deal.

CONVENTIONS

a A revoke is caused by not playing the leading suit when able to do so. It may be corrected without penalty before the trick is turned over. Penalty points can be demanded if the trick has been turned over. The whole hand is abandoned for a new deal if both partnerships revoke.

b A card exposed when not being played must be left face up on the table. The opposition then call at their discretion for it to be played during the hand. It may not be used to make a revoke.

Common techniques

a Finessing by playing the third highest of a suit when also holding the highest

b Leading with a trump when holding five or more

c Leading the fourth best of the longest suit

d Showing that ace is held by leading K

e Playing low as second player and high as third player

SCORING GAME POINTS

Game points can be won from tricks, honour cards and penalties. Partnerships keep a record of the number of tricks made in each hand. The first six tricks do not score.

Tricks seven to thirteen score one game point each, for example:

Tricks in each hand: 6 7 2 10 8 4 etc.
Game points from hand: 0 1 0 4 2 0

From this stage onwards scoring systems differ. The two most common are described here.

The seven-point game is used in America. In addition to points from tricks, partners who revoke give the opposition two game points. The final score for each game is the difference between seven and the losers' total. The final hand, after seven points have been reached, is usually played out and the additional points added to the final score.

The five-point game is used in English whist. In addition to points from the seventh trick upwards, there are points from honours, revokes and winning games.

a Four points are gained by partnerships holding all four honour cards, which are ace, K, Q and J of trumps. Two points are gained by holding any three honour cards.

Trick points take precedence over honour points if both partnerships reach a score of five points in the same deal. At the end of the game, the losers' honour points, if any, are discounted.

b Revokes attract three penalty points, allotted according to one of the following alternative rulings which must be agreed for the whole match:
   i)   three points are lost by the revoking couple;
   ii) three points are gained by their opposition; or
   iii) three points are transferred from the revokers to the opposition.

c A game is declared when a partnership gains five points.

The hand may be played out for additional points. The winners of the game get three extra points if opponents have a nil score; two if opponents have one or two points; and one if opponents have three or four points.

WINNING THE MATCH

Three games make a rubber. If the first two games are won by the same partnership, the third game is not played. The partnership winning two games gets two extra points towards their final score.

The match is won by the partnership with the highest points total at the end of a rubber.

Glossary

Boodle Cards carrying counters.

Canasta Name of a game and of a meld of seven cards of the same rank made in that game.

Carte blanche A hand containing no court cards.

Court cards The K, Q and J of each suit.

Cut Dividing a deck of cards into two parts after a shuffle, reversing the position of the two parts before dealing. Also a deck can be cut into several parts for making decisions by comparing the rank of cards revealed in the cut.

Deal The method of giving players cards.

Deck Playing cards used for a particular game.

Deuce The two of each suit.

Discard Card thrown away on the discard pile.

Following suit Playing a card of the same suit as the previous one.

Go knocking To be unable to play a card.

Hand The cards dealt and the play using those cards.

Leading suit The suit of the first card played.

Meld A group of cards of the same rank or in sequence. Also, to lay out a group of cards or add one or more appropriate cards on an existing meld.

Misdeal To deal cards incorrectly.

Packet A group of two or more cards dealt together.

Pass When a player does not play or bid.

Piquet deck When all cards below the 7s are removed from the standard 52-card deck to form a 32-card deck.

Rank Order of cards or suits in play. Higher ranks take precedence over lower ranks.

Revoke Failure to follow suit.

Sequence A run of cards of the same suit.

Setback Penalty for not fulfilling a bid (of tricks).

Slam Winning of all tricks by one player or side.

Stock The cards remaining after the deal, used later in the game.

Stripping Removing certain cards from a standard deck of 52 cards.

Suit Clubs, spades, hearts or diamonds.

Trey The three of each suit.

Trick A group of cards, one from each player in turn according to the rules of the game.

Trump A suit that outranks all others. A trump card outranks any card from a plain suit.

Upcard A card that is turned up, from the deal or the stock, to start a discard pile or to designate trumps.

Wild card A card that can be used to replace any other card – e.g. joker and 2s are wild cards in canasta.